THE Metal Craft BOOK

THE Metal Craft BOOK

50 Easy and Beautiful Projects from Copper, Tin, Brass, Aluminum, and More

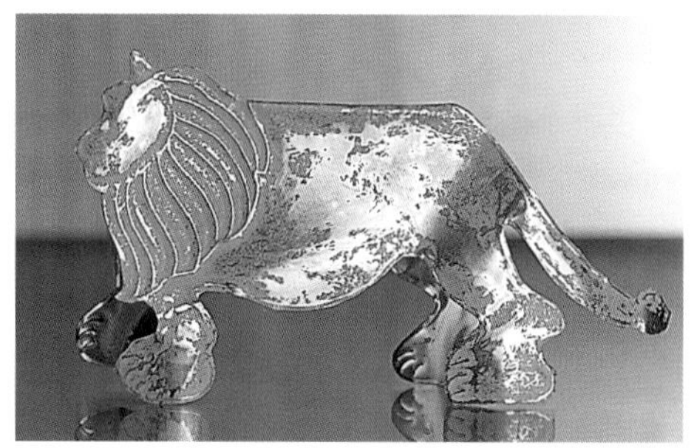

Janice Eaton Kilby and Deborah Morgenthal

A Division of Sterling Publishing Co., Inc.
New York

Art Direction and Production: **Celia Naranjo**
Computer Illustrations and Production Assistance: **Hannes Charen**
Assistant Editors: **Heather Smith and Catherine Sutherland**
Photography: **Sandra Stambaugh**
Illustrations: **Olivier Rollin**

Library of Congress Cataloging-in-Publication Data
Kilby, Janice Eaton, 1955-
The metal craft book : 50 easy and beautiful projects from copper, tin, brass, aluminum, and more / Janice Eaton Kilby and Deborah Morgenthal.— 1st ed.
p. cm.
ISBN 1-57990-170-0 (hardcover) 1-57990-310-X (paperback)
1. Metal-work—Amateurs' manuals. I. Morgenthal, Deborah, 1950- II. Title.

TT205 .K52 2000
745.56—dc21

00-037110

10 9 8 7 6 5 4 3 2 1

Published by Lark Books, a division of
Sterling Publishing Co., Inc.
387 Park Avenue South, New York, NY 10016

Distributed in Canada by Sterling Publishing,
c/o Canadian Manda Group, One Atlantic Ave., Suite 105
Toronto, Ontario, Canada M6K 3E7

Distributed in the U.K. by:
Guild of Master Craftsman Publications Ltd.
Castle Place, 166 High Street, Lewes East Sussex, England BN7 1XU
Tel: (+ 44) 1273 477374, Fax: (+ 44) 1273 478606,
Email: pubs@thegmcgroup.com, Web: www.gmcpublications.com

Distributed in Australia by Capricorn Link (Australia) Pty Ltd., P.O. Box 704, Windsor, NSW 2756 Australia

If you have any questions or comments about this book please contact:
Lark Books
67 Broadway
Asheville, NC 28801
(828) 236-9730

Manufactured in China

ISBN 1-57990-170-0 (hardcover) 1-57990-310-X (paperback)

Table of Contents

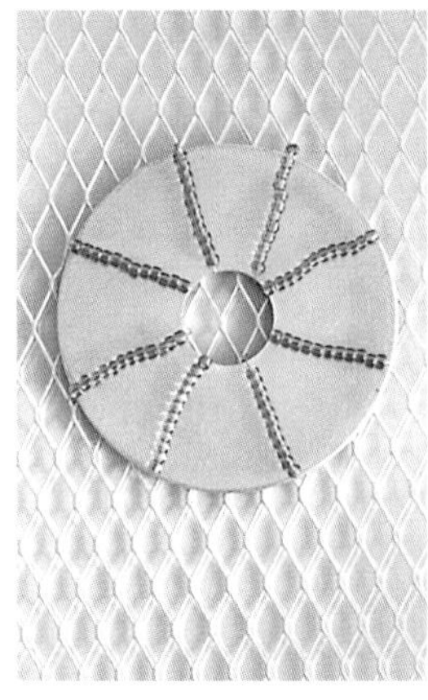

Introduction

When we think of metal, we think of beautiful objects in our streets, homes, and offices that reflect a contemporary and modern spirit. But metal has an ancient history, too. Copper and tin have been used since prehistoric times. The Egyptians treasured mirrors crafted from highly polished copper, and the remains of old Roman tin mines can still be found in England. Up until the time of the Industrial Revolution in the 19th century, sheet metal had been slowly and laboriously hand-hammered. When processes were invented for its mass production, the presence of metal products in our lives expanded exponentially.

Today we're coming full-circle, as more and more people discover the pleasures of handcrafting metal objects and the satisfaction of creating unique accessories that reflect the originality of their makers. Working with metal doesn't have to be scary or intimidating, and it emphatically does not require you to have the build of a big, burly blacksmith. Even if you don't know much about metal and you've never used it before as a creative material, this book is designed to give you the information and instructions you need to craft with metal beautifully, confidently, and easily.

The 50 how-to projects in this book will help you create attractive and useful objects from sheet metals and foils in copper, aluminum, brass, tin, and pewter, along with metal mesh, tin cans, flashing, wire, ready-made objects, recycled materials, and found metal. In addition to covering what you need to know about your raw materials, we'll review useful tools and basic techniques for working with metal. You'll learn how to mark, drill, cut, smooth, bend, and form metal. Simple joining processes such as pop riveting and soldering will be explained. You'll also learn easy ways to decorate metal with techniques such as hammering, punching, piercing, stamping, and embossing, and the use of surface decoration such as paint and patinas. The projects themselves don't require any special expertise in metals. You only need curiosity and an appreciation for the beauty of the material, plus some arts and crafts supplies, basic hand tools, everyday household items, and a few specialized but relatively inexpensive tools. As you continue to explore crafting with metal, you may want to acquire some additional tools for your work. We'll tell you about those, too.

We hope this book demonstrates that when it comes to metal you're literally surrounded by an abundance of raw material that can be used to express your own personal creativity. We hope the projects in this book inspire you to see your surroundings and all the things in it with fresh eyes. And we hope you have fun!

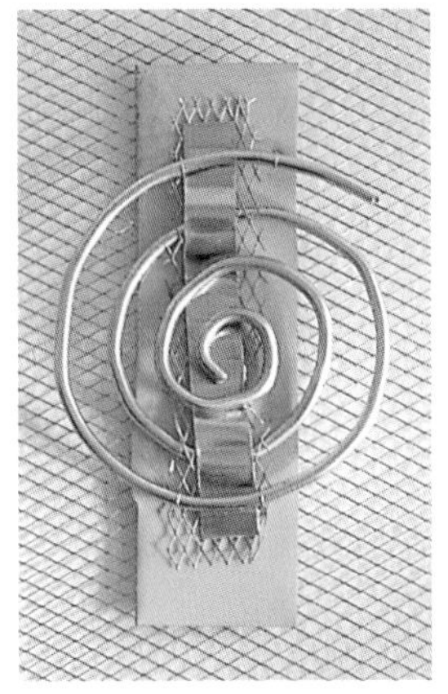

Understanding Metal as a Material

When it comes to processes such as heating, bending, cutting, joining, or coloring, every metal has its own nature, and that influences what you can do with it. Copper, tin, and aluminum are *base elements*. They're essential forms of matter that can't be created from other materials, and they each have different characteristics. Tin by nature is very malleable, and copper is very reactive to heat. Brass and pewter are *alloys*, meaning they're mixtures of two or more different metals. Brass is made of copper and zinc, and pewter is traditionally made of tin and lead, though lead-free substitutes are now used.

Knowing the composition of metals gives you clues about how they'll react to different processes. You can color brass the same way as copper, for example. There are practical limits to the thickness of metals you can craft by hand, so it's helpful to understand how their thickness is measured. If you want to use thicker metal, you can take it to a professional metal fabricator to do the cutting or forming you want. However, the good news is there's an amazing variety of metal available that can be handcrafted with simple tools at home, plus scores of ready-made metal components and objects you can use for your projects. It's easy!

How Different Metals Are Measured

It's useful to know that there are a few quirks in the way metals are measured. The *gauge* of a piece of metal indicates its thickness, but it's an inverse relationship, meaning the higher the gauge number is, the thinner the metal. The lightest sheet metal is 30-gauge; material lighter than that is generally categorized as foil. On the other end of the scale, once sheet metal exceeds a 10-gauge thickness (about ⅛ inch or 3 mm), its thickness is expressed in fractions of an inch. Some metals, including aluminum, are measured in thousandths of an inch, and the fraction is expressed as a decimal. Copper is measured by ounces (or grams) per square foot, or by decimal inches. Another quirk is that two sheets of the same metal, with the same gauge number, may have slightly different thicknesses if they come from different manufacturers. Refer to the chart on page 141 for comparative systems of measurement of common sheet metals and wire.

Metal Foils

Foils are classified by gauge, or mils (thousandths of an inch) expressed as a decimal. Foil with a .003 (three mils) thickness is 40-gauge and considered lightweight. Medium weight foil has a thickness around .005 (five mils). Craft retailers and catalogs sell *tooling foils* in a range of colors, in sizes like 9 x 12 inches square (22.9 x 30.5 cm). Mail-order suppliers also sell 36, 38, and 40-gauge foils, in 12- and 16-inch wide (30.5 and 41.9 cm) rolls that are five, 10, and 25 feet (1.5, 3, and 7.5 m) long. They're available in aluminum, brass, copper, and pewter. Foil is easy to score, cut, emboss, texture, wrap, and crumple.

Aluminum

The thickness of aluminum sheet is measured in thousandths of an inch, expressed in decimals. You can cut it by

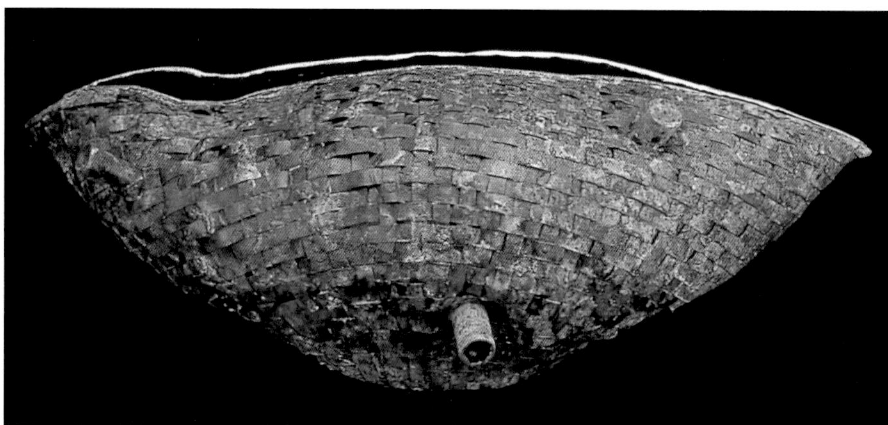

David Paul Bacharach, Bird II, *1998, 6 x 3 x 1¾ ft. (180 x 90 x 52.5 cm); copper, brazed bronze; woven, constructed, formed, patinated. Photo by Jerry White*

hand with metal shears up to 14-gauge (.0641, or $^{64}/_{1000}$ths of an inch). It continues to increase in gradations of thickness up to .090 (about 11-gauge). After that, it's measured in fractions of an inch. Roofers use *flashing* to divert water from roof joins when they lay shingles; it's a common and useful form of aluminum sheet for metal craft. Flashing will bend, but it's soft, brittle, and breaks when repeatedly stressed. Score it carefully and when you fold it, make folds by hand that are more like soft bends than sharp creases.

Brass

Brass is an alloy of copper and tin, and the sheet is measured the same way as aluminum. The maximum thickness you can work by hand is 22-gauge or .032 ($^{32}/_{1000}$ths of an inch). Brass is closer to steel than to copper by nature. It's harder to cut than copper, more brittle, and needs to be heated to stay soft during repeated hammering. Avoid using it for projects that require a lot of bending or manipulation.

Copper

Copper is very popular with crafters and metal artisans because it's easy to work with, and sheet is classified by its weight in ounces per square foot. The 16- and 18-ounce (448 and 504 g) varieties of sheet are widely available and are used for gutters, roofs, and flashing. Different weights can be translated to gauge numbers, and their thicknesses measured in fractions of an inch, but these equivalencies can vary from manufacturer to manufacturer. Simply remember that as the gauge number gets lower or the number of ounces per square foot increases, copper sheet gets thicker and more difficult to work with. You can most easily cut it with metal shears and work it with hand tools up to the 18-ounce (504 g) weight.

Copper sheet is made in different degrees of flexibility. Half-hard copper is used for flashing and gutters, and it's the most desirable for metalwork. It holds its shape, but it's malleable enough to bend. You can easily heat it with a small propane hand torch to make it softer.

Pewter

True pewter is an alloy of tin and lead. Lead and lead fumes are toxic, making it hazardous for you to heat or solder. Substitute alloys called lead-free pewter are available from craft suppliers and specialty metals distributors. You can buy them in foil and sheet form, and they can be embossed, cut, formed, or soldered. Lead-free pewter sheet is available in 16-, 18-, 20-, and 22-gauge thicknesses. Sixteen-gauge pewter sheet is .050 inches thick (0.127 cm), and that's twice as thick as 22-gauge, which is .025 inches (0.06 cm).

Rudy Rudisill, FS939, *1999, 77 x 22½ x 17½ in. (195.6 x 57.2 x 44.5 cm); galvanized steel; formed, rolled, riveted, acid patinated, waxed. Photo by Rudy Rudisill*

Chris Ake & Rhonda Kuhlman, Tooled Magnets, *1993-2000, 3½ x 3½ in. (8.9 x 8.9 cm); recycled soda cans, photocopied bottlecap images, glitter, resin, magnets; handtooled, punched. Photo by Sandra Stambaugh*

Steel

You may use some recycled "found" steel for a project. You can cut steel with shears and work it with hand tools up to a 20-gauge thickness, which is between 3/100 and 4/100 inch thick. There are several different kinds of steel: galvanized, which is coated with zinc; cold-rolled steel, which is tough and hard to work; and hot-rolled mild steel, which is the easiest to work with when using hand tools.

Tin

Galvanized steel replaced sheet tin in many applications decades ago. Tin is making a comeback among handcrafters because it's softer than copper and easily cut and worked. The preferable weight is 30-gauge.

You can obtain 1/16-inch-thick (1.6 mm) tin plate (a sheet of steel dipped in a coating of tin) in 26 x 36-inch (66 x 91 cm) pieces from art and lithography supply companies. Tinsmith suppliers sell various plate sizes, including 10 x 14 inches (25.4 x 35.6 cm). Canneries are sources for sheet tin, and you can ask furniture restorers where they obtain material for punched metal panels. Lighter-gauge Mexican tin, if you can find a source, is available in 30 x 30-inch (76.2 x 76.2 cm) or 36 x 36-inch (91.4 x 91.4 cm) sheets. Galvanized tin is coated with zinc; don't try to solder it.

Tin cans actually are made of a thin-gauge steel plated with tin, and they're easy to cut and shape by hand. Test cans with a magnet. If the magnet doesn't stick, the can is aluminum. Used tin can be beautifully recycled, as in the Gathering Love Antique Ceiling Tin Basket on page 83. The retro look of stamped tin ceilings has been increasing in popularity in interior decoration, but modern reproductions are now made of aluminum.

Hardware Cloth and Wire Mesh

Hardware cloth is a woven or welded steel mesh that's been galvanized (dipped in zinc). The openings in the cloth range from 1/8 inch to 1 inch wide (3 mm to 2.54 cm), and you can cut it with wire cutters, shape it as you would an extremely stiff, coarse cloth, and "sew" it by linking the perforations with a continuous piece of wire. Wire mesh is a woven wire cloth; its openings can be much smaller than hardware cloth (even small enough to catch bacteria!), or up to 6 inches (15.2 cm) each, which would fall apart if you tried to cut it. It's classified by the gauge of the wire used to make it, and the size of its openings. Mesh is available in steel, copper, brass, and aluminum.

Expanded Metals and Perforated Metals

Expanded and perforated metals are sheet metals that have a regular pattern of perforations punched in them.

Chester Old, Karen *(basket), 1996-99, 9 x 23 x 6 in. (22.9 x 58.4 x 15.2 cm); machine knitted stainless steel, anodized aluminum; cut, punched, bent, riveted. Photo by Jerry Burns*

Kathryn Arnett, Basket, *1994, 12 x 19 x 19 in. (30 x 47.5 x 47.5 cm); expanded steel, mining drills, metal shavings, baling wire, rebar; fabrication, soldering. Photo by Sandra Stambaugh*

Expanded metals are stretched so the openings expand to a diamond shape, while the round holes in perforated metal are left "as is." Their patterns can lend an attractive, contemporary look to a metal project.

Wire

A mind-boggling variety of wire, ranging from bulky 10-gauge to "hair" wire, is sold by the roll by hardware stores, electrical suppliers, and craft retailers. Wire is sized by gauge numbers, too. As the wire's diameter increases, the gauge number gets smaller. Wire is available in various alloys of steel, iron, copper, brass, and aluminum. A whole spectrum of decorative, colored wire is available from craft suppliers in gauges ranging from 14 to 38 gauge. You also can use a wire-stripping tool to strip heavy-gauge copper wire out of grounded electrical cable and shape it with needle-nose pliers, as you'll see in the Copper and Tin Mobile on page 112.

Where to Find Metals

In addition to foils, wire and lightweight sheet are sold by craft stores, mail-order, and Internet retailers. You can buy sheet metals, perforated and expanded metals, metal meshes, hardware cloth, rod, pipe, and wire from hardware stores and metals distributors. Industrial suppliers usually deal in large quantities such as full pallet loads, but some distributors sell smaller quantities to retail customers. If you like the look of a metal that's being used for functional or decorative purposes, you often can track down the source by inquiring at the business that fabricated or installed the object. Roofing, siding, and gutter suppliers are excellent sources. The Cosmic Copper Relief Table on page 38 uses 16-ounce (448 g) copper roof flashing, for example. Heating contractors are a good source of galvanized tin.

Off the Shelf

Once you start looking with the eyes of a metal crafter, you'll find loads of ready-made materials in everyday places. Stay alert at the grocery for cans with attractive ridge designs and fun printed imagery to create projects such as the Perk-Up Coffee Cup Napkin Rings on page 48. Check out kitchenware stores for aluminum and steel baking pans, gelatin and candy molds, and tart pans that you can solder or pop rivet to make footed bowls, candleholders, and mobiles. You actually use kitchen cutlery and a steel scrubbing pad to create the Kitchen Angel on page 44, and the fabulous Dragon Box on page 64 is made from disposable aluminum oven liners purchased at the grocery store!

Hardware stores and home decorating centers sell an abundance of ready-made metal objects that can be tweaked into entirely different and beautiful functions, too. Check out the Jester's Box on page 88, for example. Its nimble little legs are actually four robe hooks pop riveted to a copper box you make yourself, and a lamp finial serves as its decorative lid ornament. Plumbing, lumber, and carpentry departments sell hundreds of screws, caps, washers, nuts, bolts, and other connectors you can use for functional and decorative purposes. The Mud Tray Vessels on page 86 have a rather ungraceful name, but the designs' use of simple drawer pulls and glued-on washers lift plasterer's utensils to an entirely new level of easy elegance.

Off the Street

Don't overlook great sources of discarded metal that you can recycle into new life. Junkyards and auto-wrecking yards yield a huge array of metal scrap and objects to turn into wonderful pro-

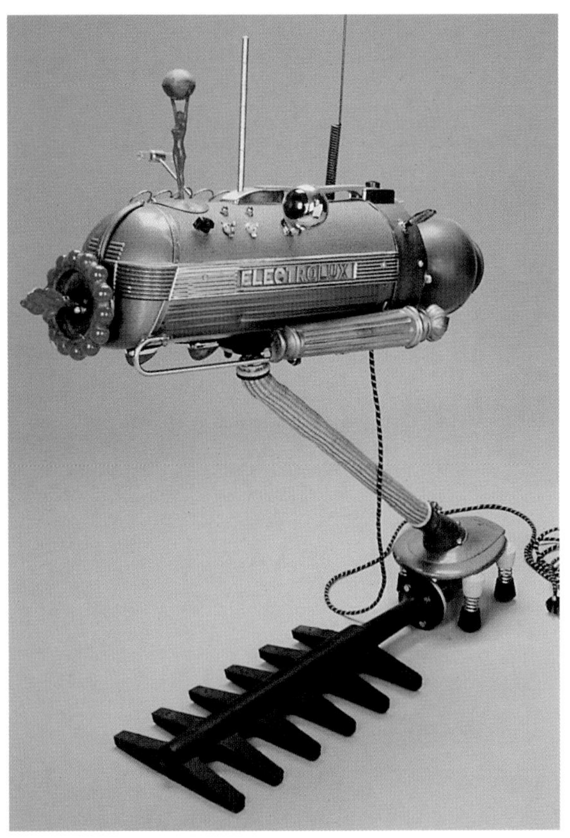

Jimmy Descant, VR-2 Deluxe Rocketship *(motorized), 1997, 39 x 11 x 36 in. (99 x 27.9 x 91.4 cm); found objects; assembled. Photo by G. Christopher Mathews*

Love Angel on page 120, but you wouldn't want to try to bend it for the base in the Rustic Moose Lamp on page 55.

Reduce, Reuse, Recycle

Think about the throwaway metal items your home or office produces every day, and how these discards can be crafted into something wonderful. Clean, used cans make a terrific and nearly inexhaustible supply of material for metal crafters, and it takes only a safety can opener, tin snips, needle-nose pliers, a file, and a little solder or pop rivets to make them into something great. Check out the beautiful Tin Can Cuff Bracelets on page 92, for example. They're incredibly easy to make! You also can ask restaurants and other food service businesses for their empty food and oil tins, which can be flattened and worked like sheet metal. The gorgeous Day of the Dead Skeleton Angel on page 126 was crafted with sheet tin from a salmon cannery.

Approach businesses that produce usable junk metals as part of their everyday operations. Your offer to take some of their waste off their hands will probably be welcome, and you'll have lots of free material. Just make sure the metals weren't used to process or to hold hazardous materials. Offset printing shops, for example, are a good source for used aluminum printing plates that are about the size of an open newspaper page. You can easily wipe the plate clean with solvent, and then paint, score, pop rivet, crumple, and even cut the material with an ordinary pair of scissors, as you'll learn when you make the stunning Woven Metal Bowl on page 74.

jects like the Phases of the Moon Pendulum Clock on page 42. Thrift stores and flea markets are a treasure trove of cookie tins and serving dishes to mine for cut-out imagery and to reconstruct into new and entirely different objects. Dumpsters in industrial parks are full of discarded steel strapping that you can pop rivet into fun containers; the Pallet Strapping Basket with Crystals on page 78 is an exquisite use of this material.

When you're choosing scrap metal for a project, think about how much bend or pressure it may have to sustain. A very rusty or brittle piece of pallet strapping won't work as a curved piece in a basket, for example, because it can't take the stress. A rusty, lacy piece of metal would make a beautiful wing for the Peace and

Miniature furniture ranging in height from 2 to 6 inches (5.1 to 15.2 cm) tall, date unknown; tin cans, sardine cans, beer and soda cans, fabric; cut, soldered, glued. Photo by Sandra Stambaugh. These tiny chairs were constructed as doll furniture, pincushions, and whimsies, and are very fine examples of a rarely found folk art.

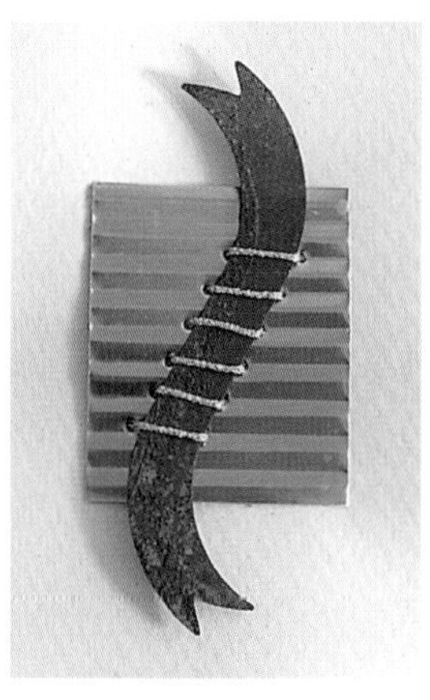

Tools and Techniques

Preparing Your Work Area

Select a sturdy table or work bench in an area with good lighting, and acquire a piece of chipboard ¾ inch (2 cm) thick to cushion your work when you drill, punch, or emboss. Accumulate magazines, a phone book, pieces of polystyrene foam, mat board, felt, and rubber to cushion your projects as you work. A couple of short lengths of 2 x 4 lumber, and wooden blocks with 45° and 90° angles, will be handy for bending metals and squaring up shapes.

You need something to hold metal so it won't move while you cut, file, or bend it. Get a small, inexpensive bench vise, or large clamps and vise grips. Clothespins and C-clamps can hold small pieces together while you work, and keep duct tape, masking tape, and electrician's tape handy for temporary attachments. If you want a very solid metal surface to hammer on, you can sometimes find small metal anvils at yard sales, or use a short section of steel girder or railroad track. If you're going to solder, stock a fireproof work mat and a fire extinguisher.

Surface Preparation

Unless you want to retain the aged look of recycled metal for aesthetic reasons, start by cleaning the metal. Metals have surface residues that can interfere with soldering, gluing, painting, or patina treatments. You need to remove any oil from fingerprints, grease from the manufacturing process, oxides from the metal's chemical reaction with oxygen in the air, and ink residues. If water beads up on the surface, it's not clean; if it sheets off, it's clean.

Clean the metal with scouring powders made with pumice, synthetic scouring pads (not steel wool), or solvents such as denatured alcohol. Afterward, handle it only by its edges. Physically scouring the surface of the metal creates *tooth*, meaning the metal has been slightly roughened, making it more receptive to bonding or decorating processes. If you're working with rusted metal, knock off excess flakes with a wire brush to help adhesives "grab" the surface.

You also may need to clean metal after soldering if it leaves discoloration or unwanted residue. This can be soaked off with a process called *pickling*, discussed on page 26 in the section on soldering.

Measuring and Marking

The measuring and marking tools you need are simple. A straight-edge metal ruler, a measuring tape, compass, fine tip permanent marker, lead pencil, grease pencil, copier paper, tracing paper, rubber cement, and dark shoe polish will all be helpful. If you start designing your own metal objects, additional helpful tools include a T-square, L-shaped metal ruler and speed square (for checking right angles), spring dividers (for measuring and transferring measurements to metal, marking circles and parallel lines), and a gauge plate (to measure the thickness of sheet and wire).

"Measure twice, cut once," is an old saying among carpenters, and it applies to metal craft, too. Work carefully when

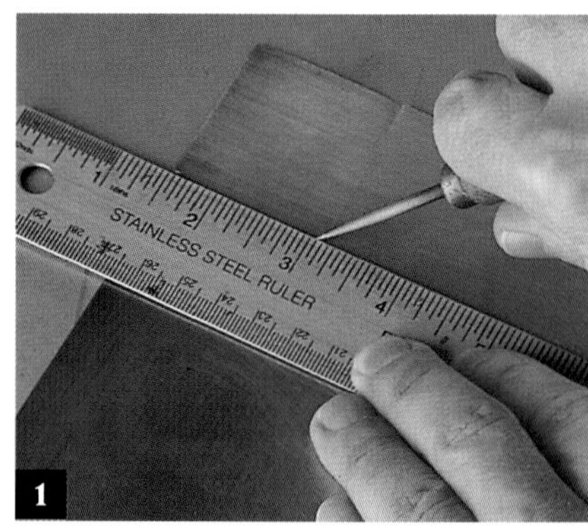

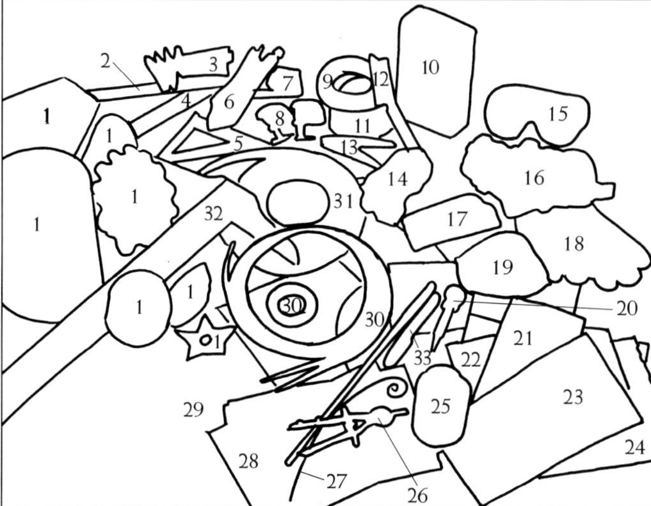

1 Raw materials
2 Steel ruler
3 Clothespins
4 Carpenter's square
5 Speed square
6 Vise grips
7 Measuring tape
8 C-clamps
9 Electrical tape
10 Solvent
11 Duct tape
12 Wire brush
13 Clamp
14 Steel wool
15 Safety goggles
16 Respirator
17 Sheet metal
18 Work gloves
19 Dust mask
20 Ball scribe
21 Metal foil
22 Tin can
23 Tracing paper
24 Hardware cloth
25 Rubber cement
26 Compass
27 Heavy-gauge wire
28 Dressmaker's carbon
29 Threaded rod
30 Steel wire
31 Trim
32 T-square
33 Permanent marker

you copy templates, or use a metal ruler to mark cutting and folding lines (photo 1). Otherwise you may cut out pieces that are crooked or the wrong size. If you score or fold some metals, such as aluminum or brass, multiple times to correct mistakes, they may crack or break.

You can draw freehand, or transfer a design template to metal. If necessary, enlarge the template on a photocopier, or transfer it to grid

Safety Precautions

The most important tool you'll need in metal working is good common sense. Always wear safety goggles and work gloves to protect yourself from metal shards and sharp edges. If you're going to bend, saw, drill, or otherwise apply force to metal, always secure it in a bench vise, clamp it to your work surface, or hold it securely with vise grips. Never put a piece of metal under stress and then cut it without being mindful of where the cut ends are going to go when the pressure is released. This counts double for springy steel materials like pallet strapping. In short, treat your materials and power tools with respect—they're stronger than you are!

Always assume that all metal edges are sharp until you've filed or sanded them. Even the newly cut edges of foil sheet or soda cans can cause an "ouch!" if you're careless. Practice good workplace hygiene by sweeping metal shavings and scraps into a container.

If you heat metals, solder, or use a lot of paints, solvents, or epoxies, work outdoors or in a well-ventilated space, and wear a respirator mask to filter out fumes. Respirators are readily available and not expensive. Don't confuse them with dust masks, which only filter out solid particles. Follow the manufacturer's directions about proper fit, and replace the filter cartridge periodically. If you want to eliminate lead fumes altogether when soldering, use lead-free solder. It's also smart to wear latex or rubber gloves when working with patinas, paints, and solvents to avoid absorbing chemicals through the skin.

Never leave a heating tool on and unattended, and always use a secure holder for a soldering tool.

paper if you need it even larger. You'll need to do this for the Day of the Dead Skeleton Angel on page 126, for example. Put a piece of white copier paper or tracing paper over the template. Trace the outline and any scoring or bending lines with a pencil or marker, using solid lines for the cut lines and dots or dashes to indicate where you bend or fold.

If you're going to use a pattern to emboss metal foil, attach the traced pattern to the foil with tape, and trace over the lines with a stylus or other pointed instrument. If you're going to cut out the pattern from metal with snips or shears, glue the pattern to the metal first with a coating of rubber cement. You also can put a sheet of carbon paper between the template and the metal (carbon side against the metal), and trace the outlines with a stylus, transferring the design to the metal.

In some projects, you'll have to *score* the pattern outline into the metal with a scratch awl, nail, or scriber as shown in photo 2. In this case, it's better to outline the template or pattern on a piece of cardboard, and cut it out with scissors or a craft knife. Attach the cardboard pattern to the metal with tape or glue, then *scribe* around it, scratching visible lines on the surface. You can apply shoe polish to the metal before you scribe, so the lines will show clearly against the polish. Cut out the pattern with shears. Remove adhesives, glues, and polish with scouring agents, cleaners, and solvents.

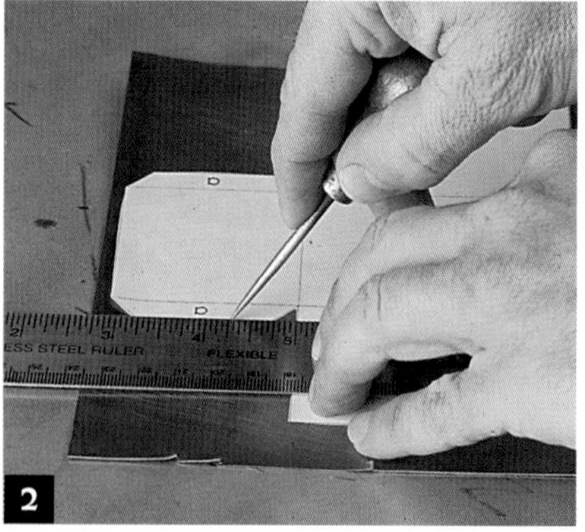

Scoring, Cutting, and Drilling

For easier bending or folding, *score* (deepen) the bend or fold lines you've drawn on the metal. Use a scribe, awl, screwdriver, or other pointed tool guided by a ruler. Experiment to see how much pressure you can apply without cutting through the material.

A pair of sharp kitchen scissors will cut foils, mesh, and metals with very thin gauges. You should use them exclusively for cutting metal. There are a few more cutting tools that will make your work easier and more pleasurable, and they're worth the investment. Quality *metal shears* with straight blades to make straight cuts are important. A set of color-coded *aviation shears* with blades curved to the right and to the left will help cut right-hand curves, left-hand curves, and circles in sheet. Buy some with compound leverage to cut metals up to 20 gauge and to maximize your hand strength.

Tin snips are smaller than shears and important for you to have; they're useful for cutting smaller shapes or cutting open tin cans, and will generally cut up to 24-gauge metal. Don't use snips on large or tough wire, solder, or the wire edge of tin cans because it can ruin them; use a pair of *wire cutters* instead. Use wire cutters to cut hardware cloth, too.

Mexican candelabra, date unknown, 18 x 14 x 14 in. (45.7 x 35.6 x 35.6 cm); tin; cut, wired, soldered. Photo by Sandra Stambaugh

3

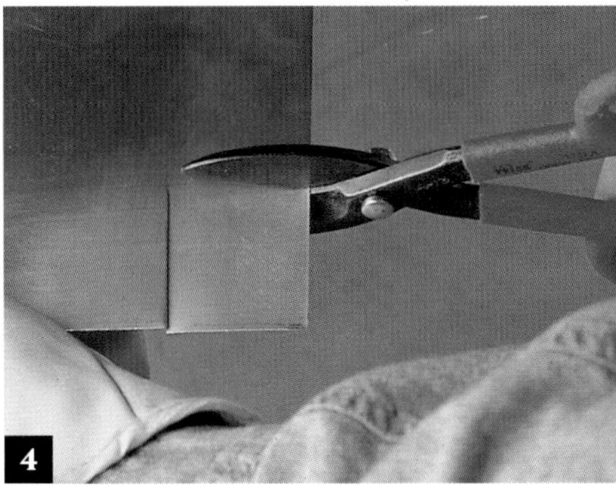

4

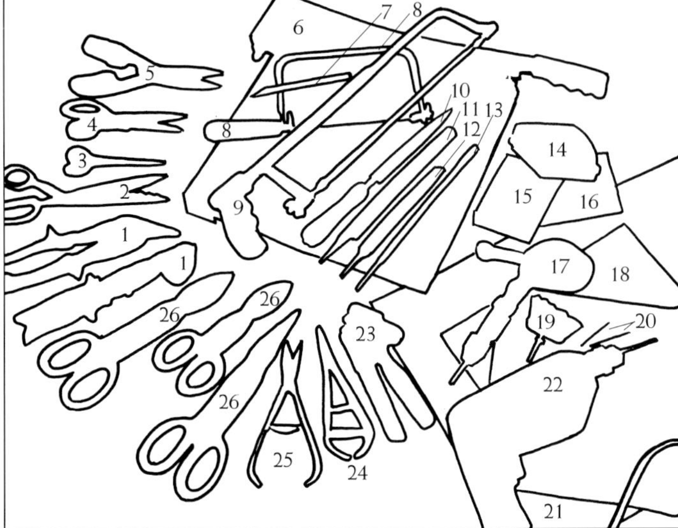

1 Aviation shears
2 Pinking shears
3 Sewing scissors
4 Scallop-edged craft scissors
5 Utility scissors
6 Guillotine paper cutter
7 Craft knife
8 Coping saw
9 Hacksaw
10 Half-round jeweler's file
11 Half-round file
12 Flat file
13 Needle file
14 Sanding block
15 Sanding sponge
16 Scouring pads
17 Hand drill
18 Sandpaper
19 Steel sanding brush for drill
20 Drill bits
21 Chipboard
22 Electric drill
23 Can opener
24 Straight cut snips
25 Curved cut snips
26 Assorted shears

With proper cutting technique, you'll avoid distorting the metal and spend a lot less time filing and sanding away jagged edges and sharp burrs. The key is never to completely close the blades when you make a cut. Before the blades close all the way, open the shears again and guide fresh metal back into the blades, never taking the shears out of the cut (photo 3). If you're cutting out an outlined shape, it can be easier to cut it out with a surrounding margin of metal first, then go back and trim it just to the right of the outline.

To cut a corner, cut one side but don't try to force the shears around the corner. As shown in photo 4, remove them from the metal and, starting from the edge of the sheet, cut to the other side of the corner and complete the second side. Take your time when you're cutting curves, and make lots of small cuts. Use the tin snips for cutting small shapes. If you're cutting small curves, a pair of hawk-billed or scroll snips can cut them without bending the metal.

When creating an intricately shaped template, it's best to drill and cut away excess material inside curves. Mark the drill point with a scribe or punch (photo 5) and position the drill at the mark (photo 6). Trim away excess material with the snips (photo 7), then file and scour the edges with a synthetic scouring pad (photo 8).

5

6

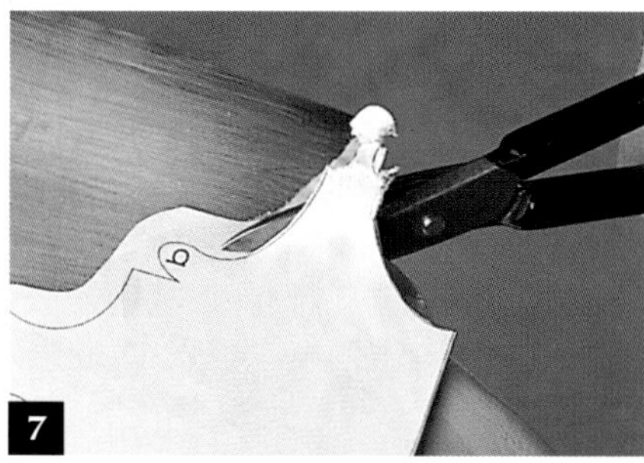
7

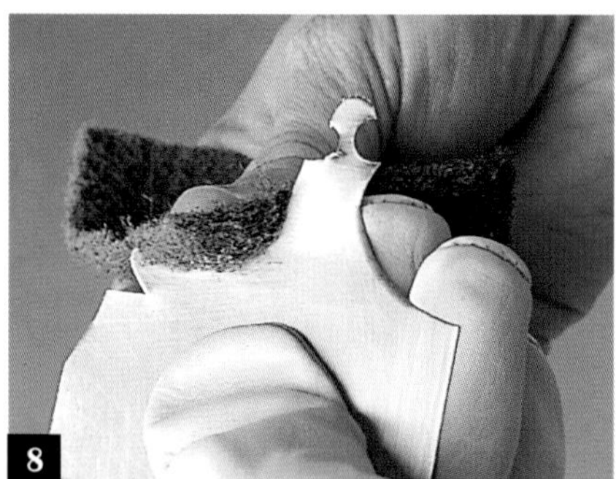
8

Use a *hacksaw* to cut sheet metals that are 14 gauge or thicker, wire rods, bar, or tubing. You can buy blades with 14 to 22 teeth per inch. Select a blade with teeth closer together than the metal's thickness, and screw it into the saw frame. Clamp the metal to the table or fix it in a vise, then put the hacksaw on the furthest side of the metal, pointing down at an angle, and put pressure on the downward stroke away from you (see photo 9). If it bends as you try to cut it, clamp it between two thin pieces of wood to stiffen it. If you're following a design on the metal, clamp the wood to the underside.

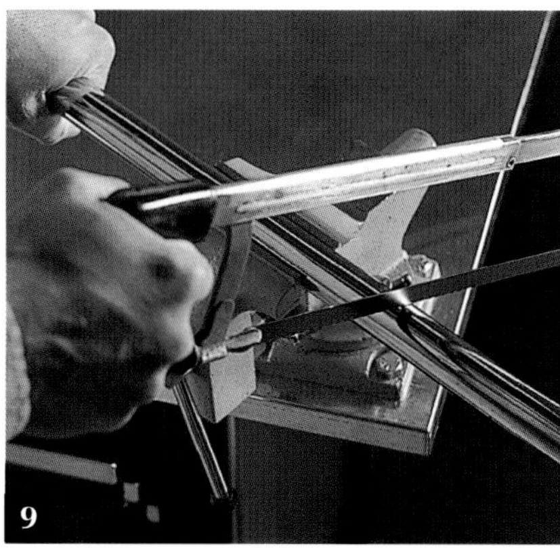
9

A *jeweler's saw* is used to cut heavy-gauge metals and holes in metal. To use one, hammer a starter depression with a punch, drill a pilot hole in the depression with a power drill, insert the saw blade through the hole and attach it to the saw frame. Then saw up and down to the edge of the hole and around its perimeter.

You'll find useful cutting tools in your home and office, too. A "safety" can opener, the type that allows you to swing the handles open to 180°, is indispensable if you want to work with tin cans. As shown in photos 10, 11, and 12, remove the top and the bottom of the can, then cut down the side with shears.

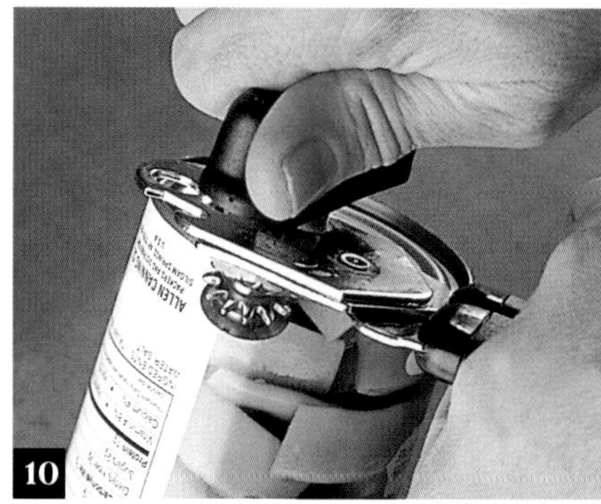
10

11

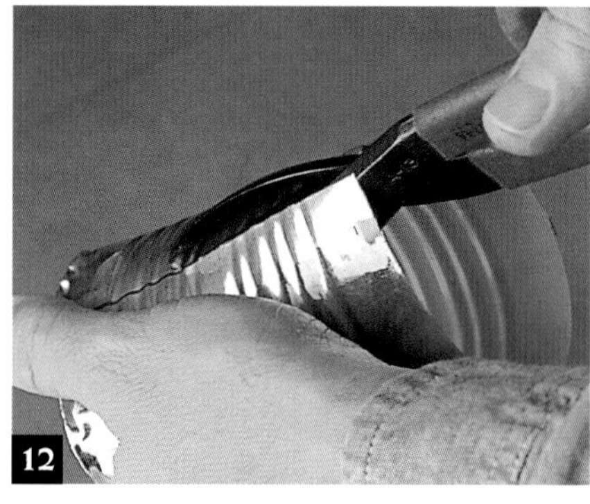
12

A 12- to 18-inch (30.5 to 45.7 cm) guillotine-style paper cutter is great for cutting used soda cans, and it works on 28-gauge or thinner sheet metal (photo 13). You also can perforate foil and thin metal with a paper hole punch. Craft stores sell a range of special scissors for cutting decorative edges in foil and light-gauge metals, and dressmaker's pinking shears can be used to good effect, too.

13

Filing, Smoothing, and Finishing

After cutting, always immediately *finish* the edges to remove sharpness. Hold the metal with a gloved hand or secure it in a vise, and use a metal file in a one-way stroke to remove jagged edges (photo 14), putting pressure on the forward stroke and lifting it on the return. There are dozens of different file surfaces and shapes (fig. 1). Flat and half-round *float files* are specifically made to work with soft metals; run some chalk over the teeth to keep them from clogging or clean them with a brush or file card. If you have a power drill, you can fit it with a grinding stone to shape or smooth edges. After filing, smooth again with abrasive cloth, silicon carbide sandpaper in assorted grits, steel wool, or synthetic scouring pads to eliminate any other burrs. To sand odd-shaped places, use a sanding sponge or wrap sandpaper around a block, piece of wood lattice, or dowel.

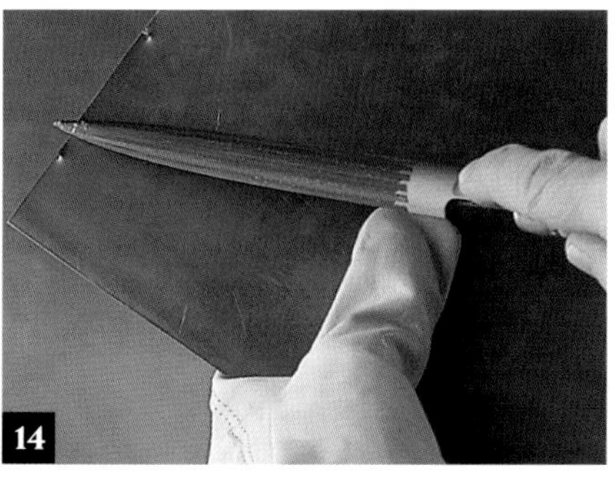
14

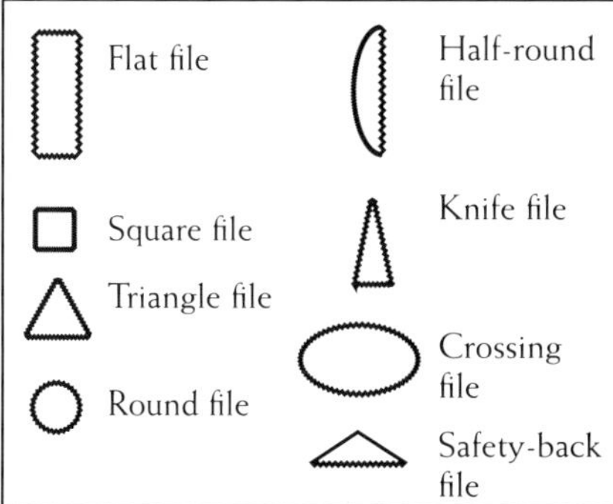

Figure 1

When you work with tin cans, file cut edges (photo 15) and scour with scouring pads. Use a pair of pliers to turn exposed edges to the inside, a bit at a time. Slip the can over a piece of PVC pipe or a wooden support such as a rolling pin and use a hammer to completely flatten the edges. You also can create a home-made safety tool for turning over can edges by filing a slot (photo 16) in the cut-off handle of an old wrench or kitchen knife. Crimp the edge to the inside with pliers or the safety tool (photo 17), put the can on a wood surface, and hammer the edge flat.

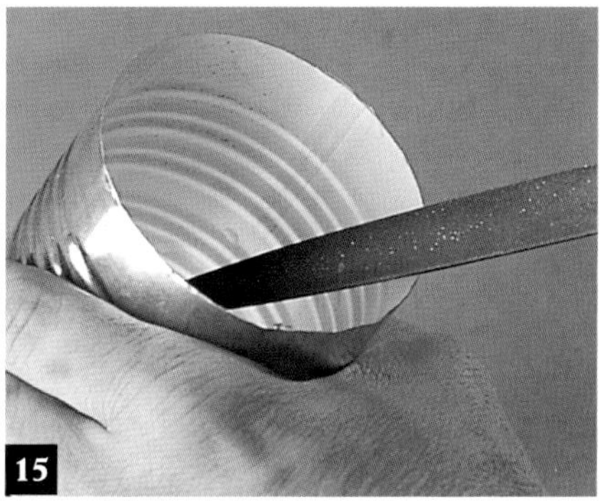
15

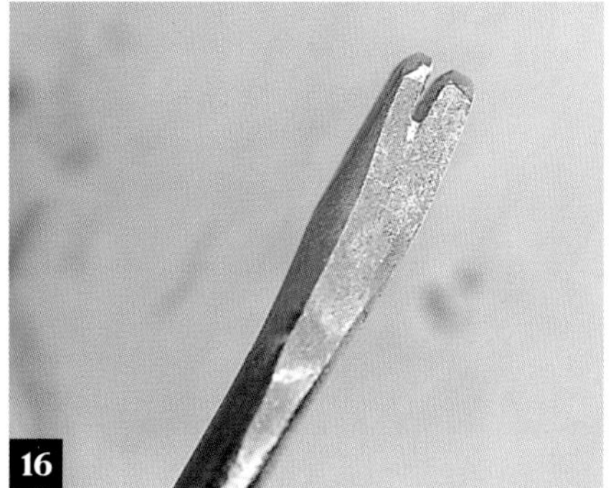
16

To finish the edges of cut wire mesh, turn over a margin of material and smooth it down with a spoon. Use wire cutters to remove stickers from the edges of cut hardware cloth.

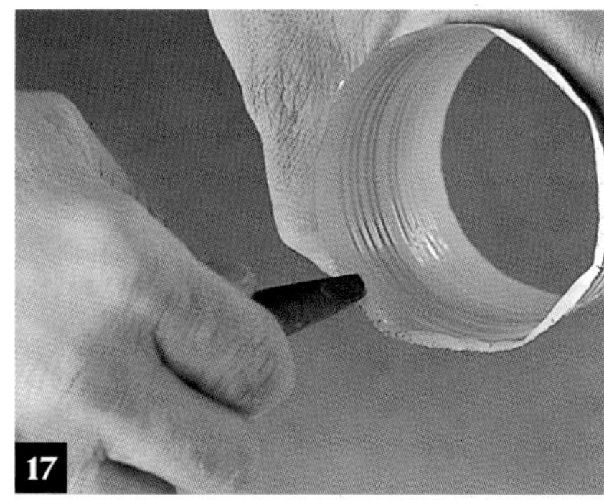
17

Making an Impression

It's easy to shape and decorate soft metal. You can hammer and bend it in different directions, mold it around objects, and pattern and texture it with hammers, chisels, and punches. All you need are a few well-chosen tools available from a hardware store or specialty tool distributor, and the imagination to see how you can use everyday objects to shape and pattern your metal.

Hammers

A regular *claw hammer* works well to *distress* metals such as aluminum flashing, making the surface appear aged. It also flattens metal folds into crisp edges, and the claw end makes attractive marks such as those on the Folded Copper Cuff Bracelet on page 104. However, one of your most valuable hammers will be the *ball-peen hammer*, which has a flat face (called the *peen*) on one end and a rounded sphere on the other end.

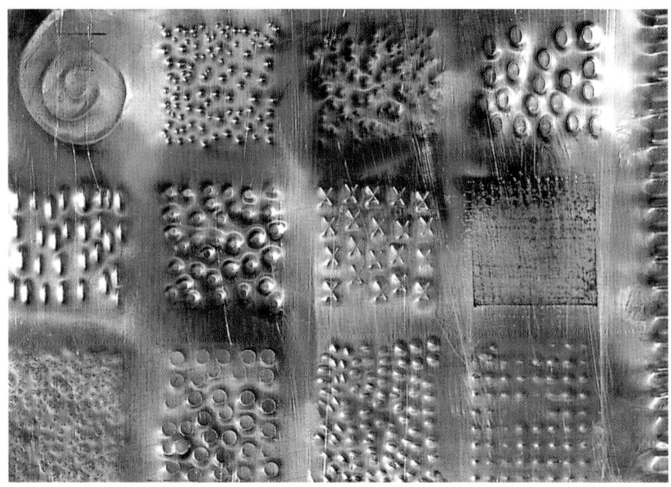
A variety of textures are easily created in sheet metal. Photo by Sandra Stambaugh

Choose a weight that feels good in your hand. The ball-peen is truly all-purpose: it flattens rivet heads, it shapes and textures (photo 18), and it strikes stamps,

punches, and chisels to pattern metal. A hide or plastic *mallet* with a 2-inch-diameter (5 cm) face is useful for shaping and forming sheet metal without leaving marks. A light *sledgehammer* or *stonemason's hammer* has the heft and weight you need to effectively stamp raised designs into sheet metal such as 16-ounce (448 g) copper. Instead of buying a specialized *planishing hammer*, you'll get the same flat-dimpled surface effect by striking a trailer hitch against the metal with a tack hammer or any hammer with a large, flat face.

Shaping and Forming

You can use the ball-peen to hammer unheated copper sheet over different sizes of PVC pipe cap, which is available from hardware store plumbing departments. This creates *dish bulges* and other domed forms that stand out in *relief* against the surface as shown in the detail below of Ivan Bailey's Cosmic Copper Relief Table.

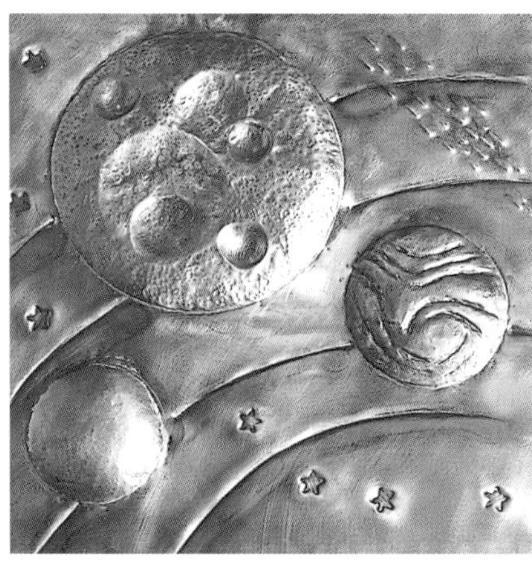

Try hammering metal sheet into a deep wooden kitchen bowl to create depressions, adapting a technique called *dapping*. As shown in photo 19, wrap the

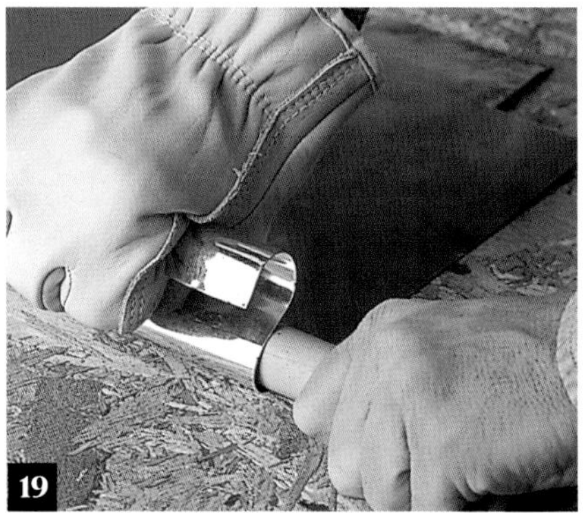

material by hand around a *mandrel* (hard cylinder or cone) such as a rolling pin, dowel, PVC pipe, or wooden spoon handle, as in the Grown Up Play Mobile on page 116. If you're feeling fancy, squeeze *metal crimpers* along the edges of sheet to flute the edge like a pie.

Bull-nose pliers, and *round-nose* and *needle-nose* pliers with box hinges, are must-have tools. You can grab and curl fringed edges of tin cans (photo 20) or wrap scrolls of sheet metal around needle-nose pliers. The Fusion Clock on page 36 is a lovely example of this technique. Needle-nose pliers can shape wire, too. Curl the wire bit by bit, keeping it flat inside the plier jaws (photo 21).

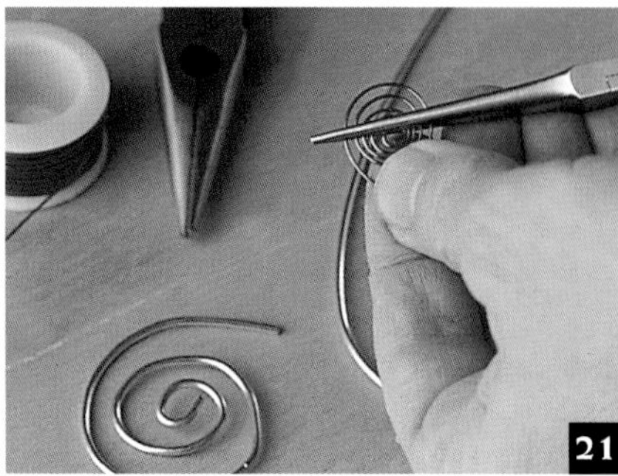

Bending

All metal will *work harden* as you bend or hammer it. The more stress it undergoes, the harder metal becomes. It's the same principle underlying the fact that a wire breaks when you bend it back and forth. Avoid this problem altogether by not overworking the metal. Try to get folds

1 PVC pipe cap
2 PVC pipe
3 Rolling pin
4 Steel letter punches
5 Plastic mallet
6 Steel mallet
7 Claw hammer
8 Ball-peen hammers
9 Mason's hammer
10 Felt
11 Needle-nose pliers
12 Jewelry pliers
13 Chisel set
14 Pliers
15 Chisel
16 Punches
17 Awl
18 Ice pick
19 Metal crimpers
20 Dressmaker's pattern wheel
21 Pizza cutter
22 Screen installation tool
23 Rubber mat
24 Metal hole punch
25 Paper hole punch
26 Surgical tweezers
27 Safety edge tool
28 Nail sets
29 Wooden spoon
30 Dowels
31 Angle block
32 Hardwood block
33 2x4 lumber section
34 Wooden bowl

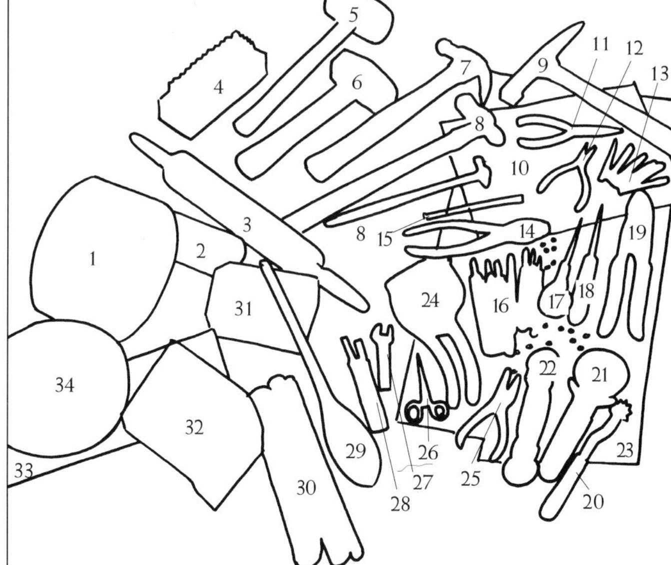

and bends right the first time, so you don't have to repeatedly stress the metal to correct mistakes.

If you're bending stiff metal or you want a cleaner right angle, "trap" the sheet between two pieces of 2 x 4 lumber as shown in photo 22, with the bend line at an outer edge of the lumber. Clamp the free end in a vise and bend it, working it back and forth a little at a time.

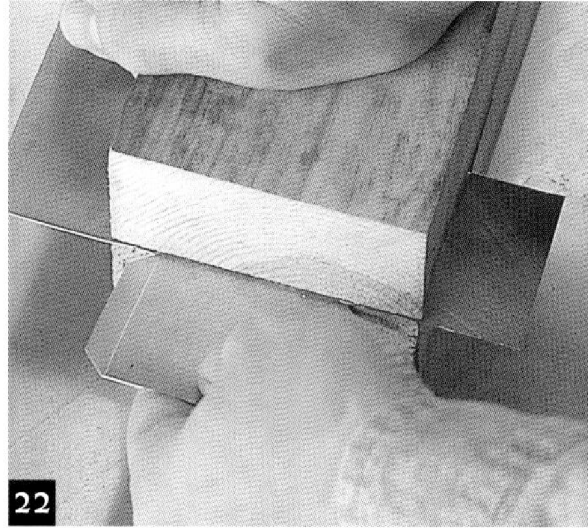
22

One technique to make clean bends in forms such as a box with tighter tolerances, uses a *chisel*. Chisels are available in a variety of cutting points, and they can be lightly hammered to create a variety of decorative marks, or struck forcefully to pierce the metal intentionally. Score the bend lines with an awl or scribing tool and place the metal on a piece of leather. As shown in photo 23, lightly hammer a blunted chisel against the score lines where you

23

want to make the bends, indenting but not piercing the metal, then bend. Try decorative chiseling with an oyster knife, wood chisels, or hobby carving tools.

Punching and Piercing

There are several kinds of punching tools, including those you invent yourself. Some *punches* are short metal cylinders in simple shapes: round, oval, square, and diamond. Place the metal on wood and position the

24

punch tip against the back or front of the metal. As shown in photo 24, strike the punch with a hammer, leaving a raised shape on the other side of the metal. Homemade punches such as screwdrivers or a set of carpenter's nails with filed-off points work well. The trio of Light Switch Plates on page 58 portray a simple yet beautiful use of this technique.

Other punches have designs engraved on the front, and they are hammered against the back of the metal with a sharp blow, raising the front. Craft suppliers sell a variety of decorative punches, such as the star shapes in the Punched Tin Lamp Shade on page 57. *Prick punches* and *center punches*, though

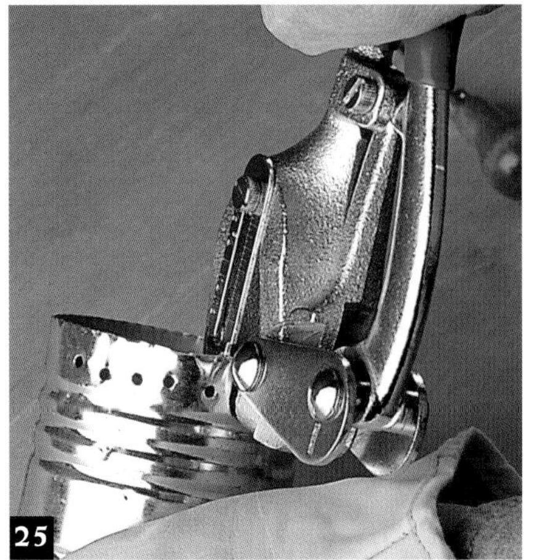
25

they're marking tools, can be hammered to make impressions and holes. Nails and bradawls can pierce metal, too. Mark them with tape so you'll hammer to a depth that produces holes of uniform diameter, and be sure to scour the holes. To create identical holes, a *metal hole punch* is a must-have tool, such as the one shown in photo 25.

Stamping

You're literally surrounded by fun objects and intriguing surfaces whose impressions can be hammered into thin metal sheet. Consider the textural possibilities of waffle irons, bricks, concrete, manhole covers, and street signs and numbers. You can experiment with making your own decorative stamps from everyday objects, such as buttons, buckles, spools, hardware, or kitchen utensils. Jewelry and metal-supply companies also sell letter and number stamps.

Embossing

Embossing is an easy technique that creates imagery and raised patterns that stand out in relief against the flat surface. It can be done on foils using simple hand tools. Take a look at the Folk Art Reindeer on page 128 to see how easy it is! Copper, brass, aluminum, and pewter foils are easily embossed. Some craftspeople find pewter to be the softest and most responsive. You can buy metal styluses with fine or blunt points in different diameters, and wooden embossing tools that are like small, slim dowels with shaped ends. Any item that leaves an impression on the foil without tearing through it is useful, such as a dried-up ballpoint pen, chopstick, or large nail

Terry Taylor, La Mano Poderosa (The Powerful Hand), *1999, 12 x 6 x 2 in. (30.5 x 15.2 x 5.1 cm); tin milagro, oil lamp reflector, tart pan; stamping, lettering, drilling, soldering. Photo by Terry Taylor*

with a filed-down point. Household items, such as a pizza cutter, screen installation tool, and dressmaker's tracing wheel, create interesting effects.

To emboss foil or metal, temporarily attach your paper pattern to the material with tape or glue (or draw it on directly), and use a metal stylus or other pointed tool to outline the design (photo 26). Work the material with a

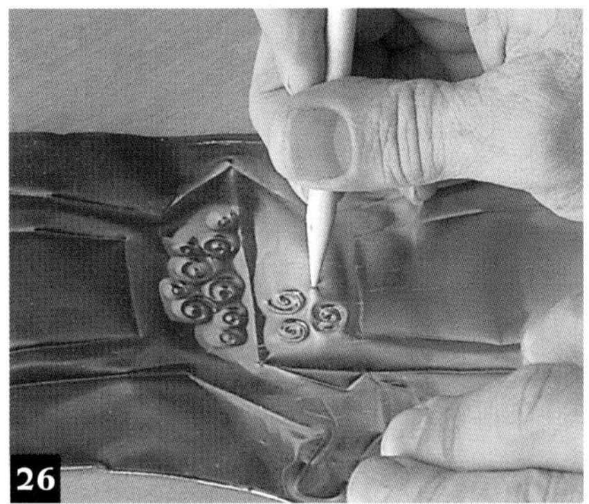

wooden embossing tool with firm, repetitive strokes in one direction. This creates depressed areas on the "drawing" side, while on the other side, the design becomes three dimensional, literally rising above the surface of the metal. The whole secret to embossing is repetition and working in stages, rather than trying to emboss with one or two strokes. Working too hard or too fast may pierce your material, particularly if you're working with a metal stylus.

Alternate the embossing between the front and back of the design, using a wooden tool inside the outlines and a metal stylus outside the outlines to give the design more dimension. Suppress any puffiness in the areas around the relief by working them with a pencil eraser or stump. As you'll see in the Miniature Armoire with Embossed Pewter Panels on page 118, it's helpful to emboss the reverse (back) side of the

design while the metal is lying facedown on a soft surface, as shown in photo 27, and to flatten, sculpt, or outline the

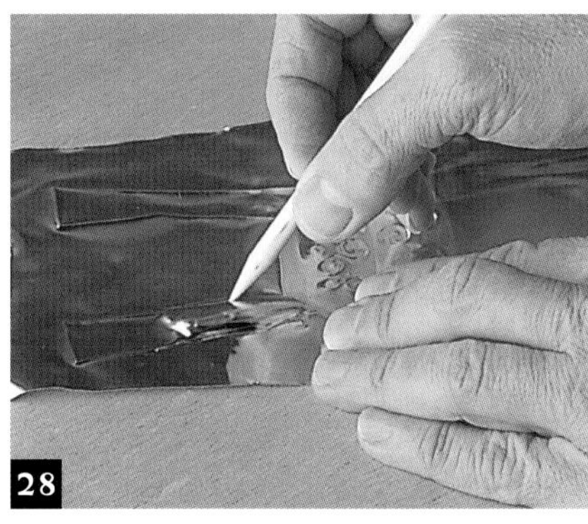

relief area with the metal right side up on a hard surface, as shown in photo 28.

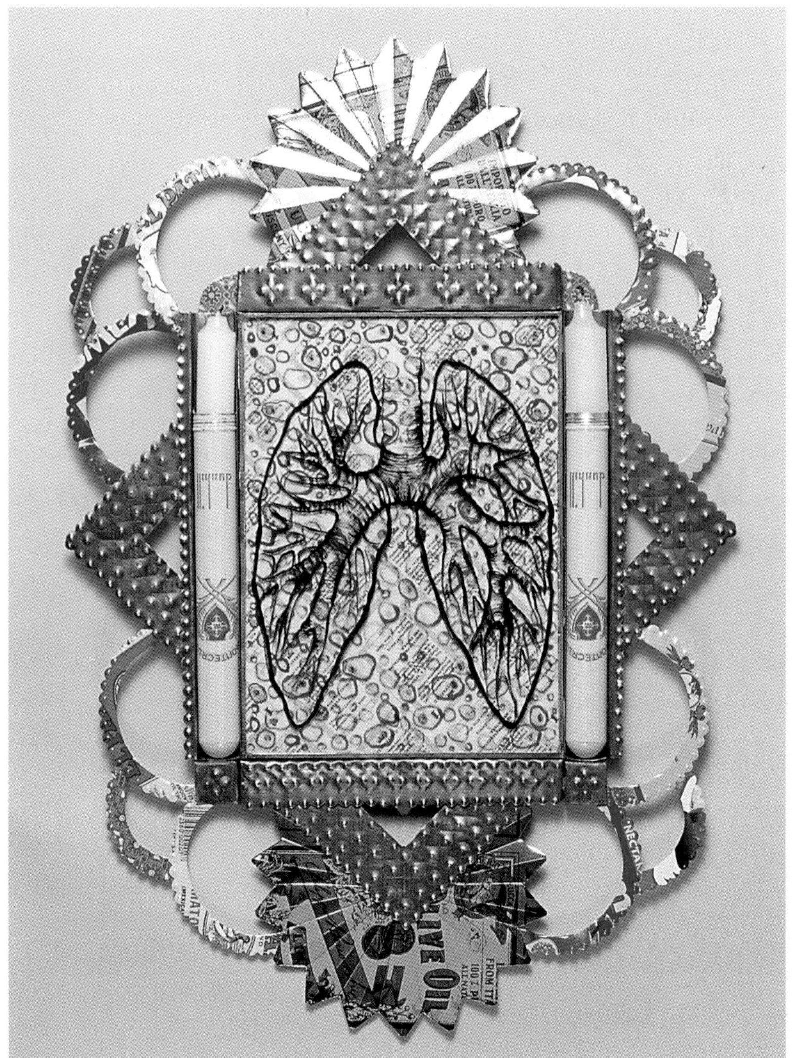

Chris Ake & Rhonda Kuhlman, Lung Retablo, *1997, 17 x 15 in. (43.2 x 38.1 cm); cigar tubes, candles, recycled roofing tin, recycled olive oil tins, paint, ink; hand tooled, scored, soldered, reverse painted glass. Photo by Chris Ake*

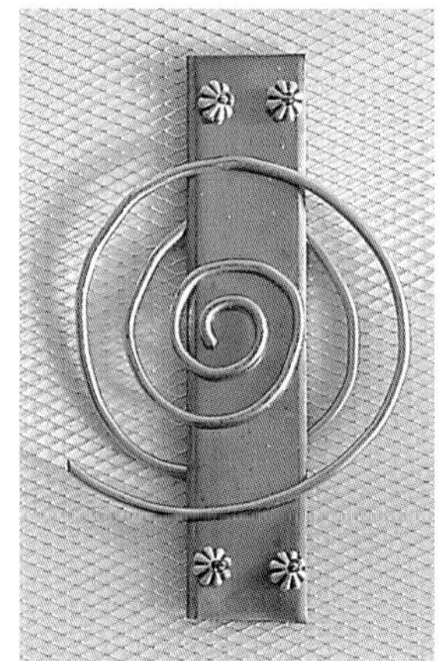

Easy Ways to Attach Metals

There are five easy "low-tech" ways to attach metal: pop riveting, soldering, use of ready-made fasteners, sewing, and gluing. *Pop riveting* joins pieces of metal with small metal pins that are permanently squeezed into place by a special tool. *Soldering* uses heat and a special meltable alloy to bond two pieces of metal. Hardware and hobby stores are full of ready-made connecting devices that, once you drill a couple of holes, attach metals in a matter of seconds. They may be the simplest solution. A *power* or *hand drill* with a variety of *drill bits* is essential to make accurately sized holes for screws or pop rivets. And finally, don't ignore all the excellent hobby glues and special adhesives made for metal.

Pop Rivets for Beginners

When it comes to joining materials, pop rivets may be your best friends. They're essential for crafting the Trapezoid Photo Box on page 67, for example, and they're easy to use. Pop rivets are stems of metal attached to metal heads. The stems fit into holes predrilled in the pieces of material to be joined. When squeezed with the specially designed *pop rivet gun*, the rivet flares and expands, flattens at one end, and breaks off, permanently connecting the material. You can

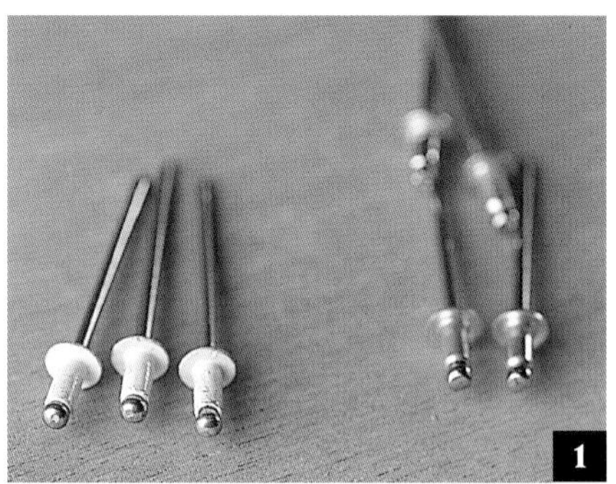

buy aluminum, steel, and copper pop rivets and a pop rivet gun at craft or hardware stores. Rivets (photo 1) are widely available in various lengths and 1/16-, 1/8-, and 1/4-inch diameters (1.6, 3, and 6 mm); 1/8 inch (3 mm) is the most popular. The most important dimension to check is the rivet's *grip range*, which needs to be a little longer than the total

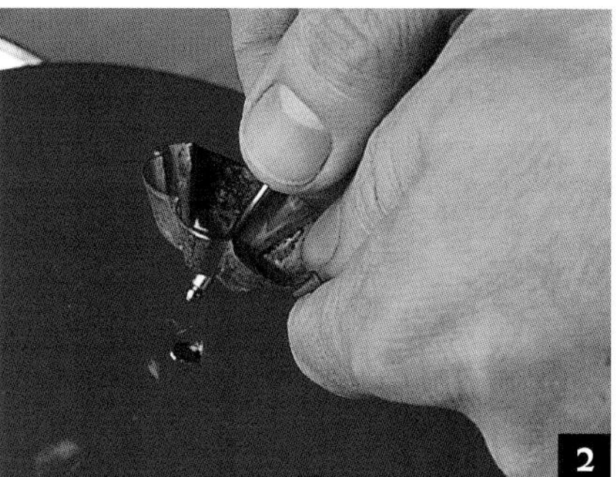

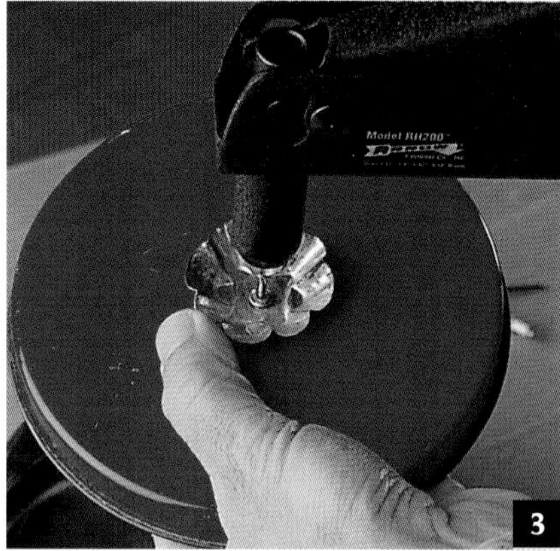

thickness of the materials you want to connect.

Here's how you pop rivet. Use an electric drill with a drill bit matching the diameter of the pop rivets, and pre-drill holes through the material to be connected. Place the pop rivet stem through the hole as shown in photo 2, making sure it's fully seated. You may have to wiggle it in, since there's not much tolerance between a stem with a ⅛-inch (3 mm) diameter and a ⅛-inch-wide (3 mm) hole. You can try putting the rivet in the gun first and wiggling it into the hole, but be careful or the gun may ratchet and spread the rivet prematurely. Apply the pop rivet gun as shown in photo 3 and squeeze it. If you want the inside end of the installed rivet to be flush with the material, place it on a hard surface and rap the rivet with the ball end of a ball-peen hammer, flattening it (photo 4).

If the rivet only pops halfway during installation, try squeezing it again with the gun. If that fails, drill out the rivet with a matching drill bit, and cut it out with snips. When you try again, either use a longer rivet, tighten up the materials you're trying to join, or put a washer on the other side. If the rivet pulls completely through soft material, put a washer on the other side of the material and re-rivet. If you pop rivet metal to a brittle material such as hard plastic, drill the holes a bit oversized, and put a washer on the other side of the plastic to absorb some of the stress so the plastic won't crack.

1 Igniter
2 Propane torch
3 Work gloves
4 Soldering gun
5 Glue
6 Cellophane tape
7 Ammonia
8 Patina solution
9 Rubber gloves
10 Foam brush
11 Paintbrush
12 1/8-inch rivets
13 Pop rivet gun
14 Fender washers
15 Nuts, bolts, split washers
16 Wire
17 Needle-nose pliers
18 Wire stripper
19 Rosin core solder
20 Flux brush
21 Flux
22 Solder
23 Soldering iron
24 Lighter
25 Matches
26 Heat-resistant pad

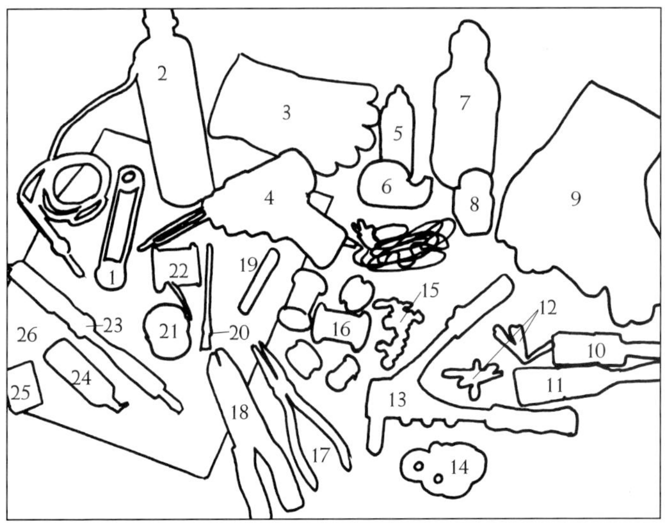

Demystifying Solder

The process of soldering doesn't have to be intimidating, or feel like a hit-or-miss process that may or may not work. In fact, it's one of the most useful and simplest ways to join two pieces of metal. Soft soldering is good for objects that won't be subjected to lots of weight or hard or repetitive stresses.

When you solder the metals covered in this book, you'll use what's called *soft*, or *com-*

Chris Ake & Rhonda Kuhlman (Recycled Works), Clock with Dice, *1999, 38 x 38 in. (96.5 x 96.5 cm); dice, brass, metal rods, neon, recycled roofing tin; handtooled, soldered. Photo by Chris Ake*

mon, solder. It comes in bars or rolls of wire (also known as *stick solder*). You'll see two numbers on a roll of wire: the first is the percentage of tin, the second of lead. The two most useful solders contain 50/50 or 60/40 tin to lead. If you can find it, a 63/37 solder has the most strength and lowest melting point of all. *Half and half* (50/50) solder melts at 450°F (250°C), while *fine* (60/40) solder melts at 390°F (217° C). If speed is important in your soldering project, melted 60/40 solder solidifies the quickest. For decorative work, 63/37 or 60/40 is good; use 50/50 for three-dimensional pieces. If you can't find 50/50 at a hardware store, it's available at stained glass suppliers. *Fluxes* are commercially-prepared pastes or liquids you paint on the join before soldering, to keep the metal from oxidizing when it's heated. Without flux, oxides will prevent the solder from "grabbing" the metals to be joined. Fluxes for specific metals are available.

Use lead-free, tin-based solders and matching fluxes for items that will hold food and drink or for jewelry to be worn next to the skin. You should also use lead-free solder if you want to solder unlike metals, such as silver plate to copper. Plumbing supply houses and hardware stores sell lead-free supplies. Lead-free solder has a higher melting point than common solder, so heat your metal quickly and don't burn up the flux, or the solder won't flow freely and you may pit the material.

How to Solder

Fit the pieces together and clamp, tape, or wire them in place with number 20 black iron binding wire. You also can buy special soldering tweezers made to withstand high heat. Scour the join and file the edges. Brush on flux at the join as shown in photo 5.

Many crafters use an *electric soldering iron* or *soldering gun*, originally designed for work with electrical components. For larger jobs or faster heating, consider using a nonelectric soldering iron called a *copper*, heated by a small handheld *propane torch* (available in inexpensive plumbers' kits at hardware stores).

Next, sand any tarnish from the electric iron point, or file the tarnish off the copper. Flux the tip. Now you'll *tin* the iron. Warm the electric iron to solder-melting temperature, or heat the copper with the propane torch. Reflux the tip. Melt a bit of solder on it and rub it over the edge, creating a layer of solder. The iron or copper is hot enough when the solder flows easily over the flux-coated areas. Wipe off excess solder. If you're using an

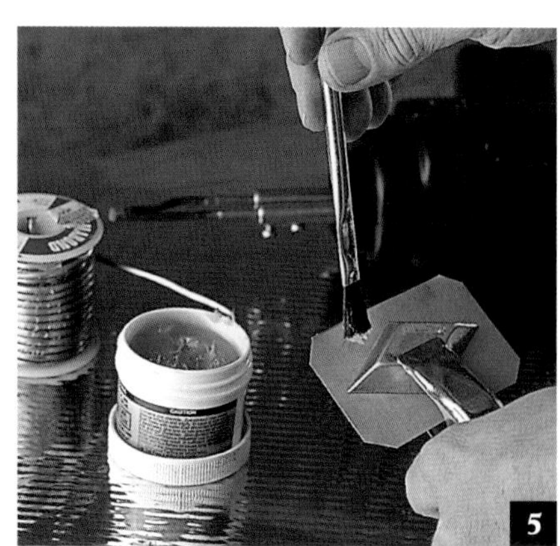

electric iron, hold the tinned point against the metal to warm it. Hold a piece of solder against the join as shown in photo 6, close to the iron, pulling the solder along behind the iron. If the iron and join are warm enough, the solder will melt and flow along the join. Touch the iron tip to a wet cellulose sponge to wipe off burned solder or flux residue.

If you're using a torch-heated copper, load the tip with solder by touching it to the wire solder. Hold the tip on the join until heat transfers to it and the solder starts to flow. Draw the iron along until you use all the solder or until the joint is completed. Repeat and add more solder if necessary. Brush on denatured alcohol with a natural bristle brush, and wipe clean with a cotton cloth.

Soldering Tips for Different Metals

Aluminum requires its own special solders and fluxes due to its particularly low melting point. It shouldn't be soldered to copper or brass; the dissimilarity of metals will create a galvanic reaction, causing corrosion similar to that on a car battery. Brass is an alloy with lots of copper; it's easy to solder and needs less heat than copper. Soft solders don't match the color of brass, so plan to either hide the joins or use the contrast decoratively. Copper is easy to solder and has good strength. On the down side, it's highly conductive and demands a lot of heat, especially if it's heavy-gauge. Consider using a handheld propane torch instead of an electric soldering iron to provide more and faster heat. Work quickly and apply flux generously. Soft solders don't match copper's color, so hide the joins or utilize the color contrast. Don't heat soft solder on copper above 500° F (260°C) or you'll pit the material. Tin is easy to soft solder, but don't solder galvanized metals; they require pretreatment with dangerous acids. Use adhesives or mechanical fasteners instead.

Common Soldering Problems

If the solder sputters and spits while you're working, trim your flux brush to ¼ inch (6 mm) and apply less flux. If a soldered area has incomplete, unsoldered patches, you could be under- or overheating. Clean the metal, re-flux, and resolder, adjusting the heat. If the solder flows to one side of the join, add more flux and reheat the join, making sure both sides of the join are equally hot. Resolder. If the solder forms into balls and won't flow, you may be trying to soft-solder galvanized steel, or you may be putting heat directly on the solder; if so, stop! Check if any adjoining wire or tools are stealing heat from the join. Clean and resolder. If the soldered join is grainy or dull looking, too little heat was used, or the join was moved before it cooled. Remove the solder, repeat, and cool completely.

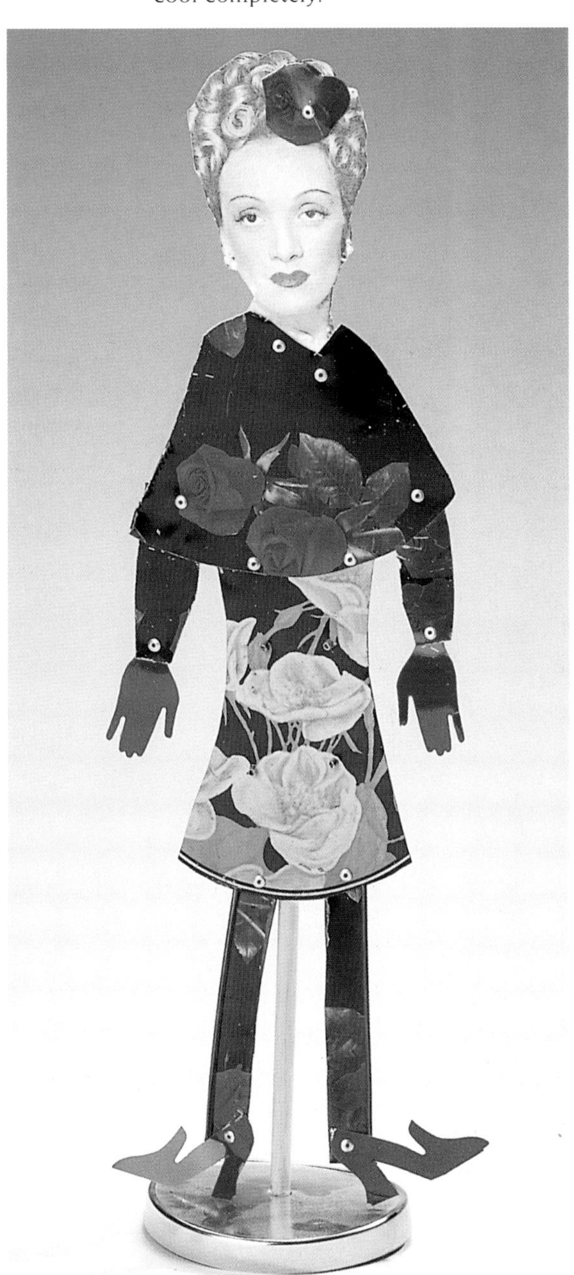

Janet Cooper, Marlena, *1998, 5 x 1 x 14 in. (12.7 x 2.5 x 35.6 cm); vintage tins, colored photocopies from vintage catalogs, rivets; die-cut, pasted/laminated, fastened. Photo by H. Goldman*

Cleaning Up after Soldering

You can remove excess solder and heat marks. Scrape off the excess by hand, scour with abrasive cloth, or file it with a float file. You also can *pickle* a piece to remove heavy discoloration or flux residue by soaking it in warm, commercially-made pickling solution, then rinsing it with water. Follow package directions for mixing and heating the solution. A heatproof ceramic container on a hot plate makes a good pickling vessel, or a crockery slow cooker (seal the seams with silicone caulk). Don't put iron objects in the pickle. Use copper, brass, or wooden tongs, and rinse pickled pieces with water. Discard the solution when it turns dark blue.

Weaving and Sewing with Metal and Wire

You can substitute heavy-gauge wire and metal strips for more traditional basket-weaving materials, such as the Woven Copper Basket on page 72, or reproduce well-known patterns, such as the Water Snake chevron weave in the Woven Metal Bowl on page 74. You may have to adapt them to allow for lesser flexibility of the metal. You also can easily incorporate metal in mixed media, woven pieces such as the Woven Copper Bookmark on page 98.

Hair wire makes a great substitute for thread, though you'll have to be careful not to knot or kink it. Try rubbing a little candle or beeswax on it to make it more slippery, and use a tapestry needle if it's helpful. Heavier wire can be used, too, to join hardware cloth and mesh. Thread it through the perforations with needle-nose pliers as in the Hardware Cloth Basket on page 70. If you want to "sew" sheet metals, punch holes on both edges and connect them with wire of sufficient gauge.

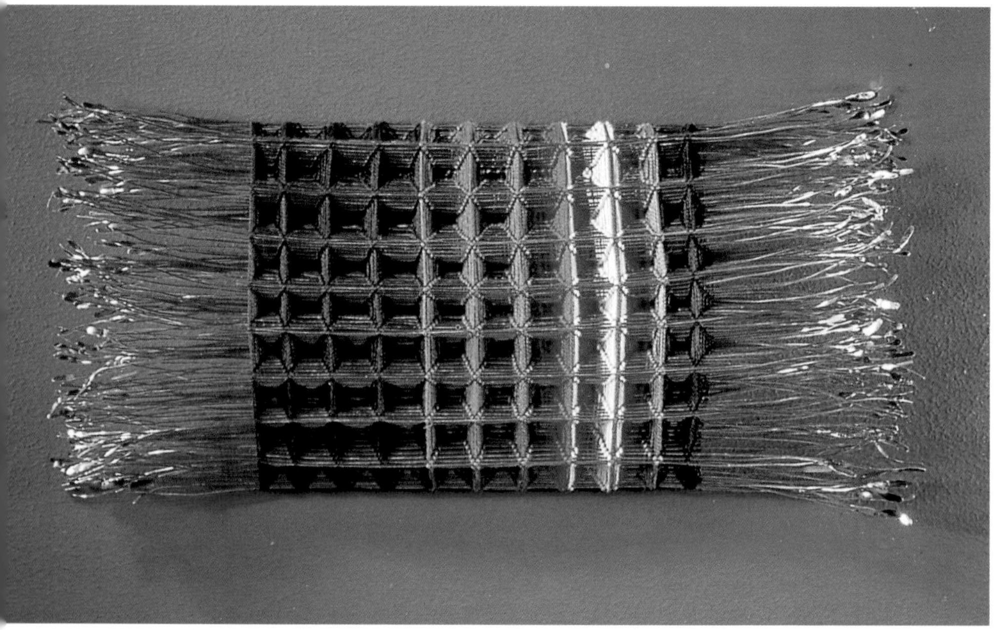

Cori Saraceni, Eclipse, *1993, 12 x 24 x 4 in. (30.5 x 61 x 10.2 cm); copper wire, colored cottons; woven. Photo by John Warner*

Using Ready-Made Fasteners

The fasteners section of a hardware store brims with useful items for connecting metals. Hobby stores or jewelry supply companies can sell you anything else you need. Jump rings, lock washers, S-joins, hinges, catches, clasps, earring and brooch backs, locks, chains, threaded rod and closures, mini-screws and nuts all can be used. For example, the gorgeous Tie Plate Candle Shades on page 60 use simple lock washers to connect perforated metal plates.

Glues and Adhesives

You don't always have to drill, weld, or solder to connect or decorate metal. Plain white craft glue works well to glue paper to metal, and an extra-tacky craft glue is good for attaching mat board or fabric. Jewelry glues will bond small pieces of metal. Cyanoacrylate glue bonds similar and dissimilar materials instantly, including your skin, so be careful using it. Two-part epoxy resin comes in two vials or syringes. Follow the manufacturer's directions to mix specific proportions of the two parts together, stirring it with a wooden tongue depressor and applying it quickly. Use it in a well-ventilated area and avoid breathing the fumes.

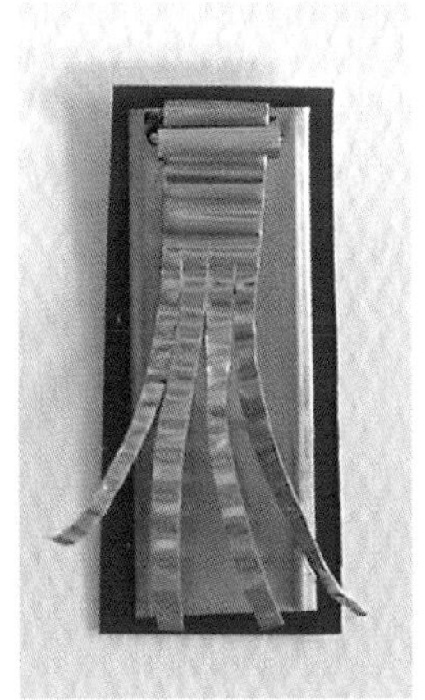

Decorative and Protective Surface Treatments

Scouring and Grinding

After you finish a metal piece, you can scour the surface with steel wool to give it beautiful, brushed highlights. A sanding bit on a power drill drawn lightly along a metal surface creates squiggles and arabesques that will shine brightly against the mat surface. This is a particularly nice effect on steel or galvanized metal.

Painting

Metal is in itself a beautiful material. Paint sparingly in a complementary spectrum, or use opaque, bright colors and simple lines to suggest folk art. If you want your metal to have an "aged" appearance, apply combinations of black, white, turquoise, metallic red, gold, and bronze acrylics. Mix it all together for muddy tones related to the color of the metal. Paint or sponge it on. Be messy, and maybe even wipe some off as you go. Acrylic craft paint is used with this technique to age the Distressed Aluminum Mirror on page 30. Experiment with enamels and acrylics, metallic sprays, translucent glass paints, and specialty texture paints from hardware and auto stores, and craft suppliers.

Before you paint, clean the surface thoroughly with soap and water, then scouring powder, and finish with a wipe down of denatured alcohol or other solvent. Let it dry. The "tooth" you create helps the paint grab the surface. Work on a flat surface to avoid runs. In some cases, you can paint the metal before you actually use it to fabricate an object, but paint last if you will hammer, stress, or solder it during construction. Use bristle or foam paintbrushes for a smooth finish. Try layering on different colors with sponges or steel wool and lightly sand selected areas for a textured, variegated surface or to highlight relief work (see photo below). Spray, stipple, or drip paint onto wet backgrounds in contrasting colors.

Seal enamel-painted pieces with polyurethane applied with a brush. Use spray-on, matte-finish, clear acrylic sealer to seal other surfaces.

Patinas

Metals form reactive residues (*oxides*) on their surfaces when they come in contact with certain chemicals or elements such as oxygen, and colored patinas are the result. For example, the beautiful blue-green patina you've admired on copper rooftops or weathervanes is actually copper rust, and the fancy name for it is *verdigris*. The same process of oxidation makes iron and steel rust. It sounds scientific, but you certainly don't have to be a chemist to use oxidation to create wonderful colors on metal. Patination is really more of an art than science, so expect the unexpected to happen!

Natural and Homemade Patinas

If you're very patient, you can put copper outdoors, leave it exposed to the elements, and wait for the verdigris to happen naturally. If you'd like to speed things up and use home-made materials, you can spray on water and sprinkle on

David Paul Bacharach, Wall Quilt Sampler, *1999, 2 x 3 ft. (5.1 x 7.6 cm); woven and constructed copper and steel; patinated. Photo by Joel Breger*

salt to produce the copper patina shown in the Dragonfly Plaque on page 51. Bury copper objects in a plastic bag of kitty litter or sawdust saturated with kitchen ammonia to create a textured rust and green patina, as shown in the Copper Fish Mobile on page 53.

You also can combine household materials in another easy process to give copper or brass a blue patina. Sprinkle water or vinegar on the metal you want to color, then sprinkle it with salt. Suspend it over a dish of ammonia or set it beside the dish, sealed inside a covered bucket or plastic bag. Let the vapors react with the metal for several days.

Heat promotes oxidation, too, and it produces particularly beautiful results on copper. A candle flame created the lovely color variations in the Woven Copper Coasters on page 32, and you can use a small propane torch to color larger pieces if you wish. You also can try heating copper in your kitchen oven at 325° to 375°F (180° to 210°C). It will go through several color changes, finishing with a bright blue within half an hour, so monitor its progress. Never leave any heating process unattended.

Off-the-Shelf Patina Solutions

If you're interested in creating your own patina solutions, you should know that chemical suppliers are increasingly reluctant to sell to the general public because of the possible misuse of their products. However, commercially prepared liquid patina solutions in green, blue, and burgundy are obtained easily from crafts suppliers. Suppliers to the jewelry industry also sell solutions that will create brown, black, brown-black, gray-black, and green patinas on copper and brass, plus a blackener for aluminum.

The green and blue solutions work on copper and brass, as in the Earrings and Brooch Set on page 110. Keep in mind that, as long as the metal you want to color contains some of the metal that reacts to a patina solution, coloration will result. The burgundy patina solution gives a brownish purple color. It's actually a suspension of iron oxide (rust!) that settles on the surface of the metal and grabs its "tooth."

Cleaning removes the oil and dirt that block the solution, and leaves bare, uncolored spots. Clean the metal surface with soap and water, then scrub it with pumice powder and water using a soft brush. Wipe down the surface with denatured alcohol and a rag, and let it dry. You're now ready to color the metal.

Applying the Patina Solutions

You can squirt or pour the patina solution on your metal surface, making sure it's well-wetted. Experiment with immersing the object, spraying on the solution from a spray bottle, or sponging or brushing it on. You can let items sit in the solutions overnight in a jar or ceramic dish. You also can experiment with layering or developing the patina gradually. Dilute the solution, warm the object in hot water, dip it for a few seconds at a time in the solution, then rinse. Let it dry.

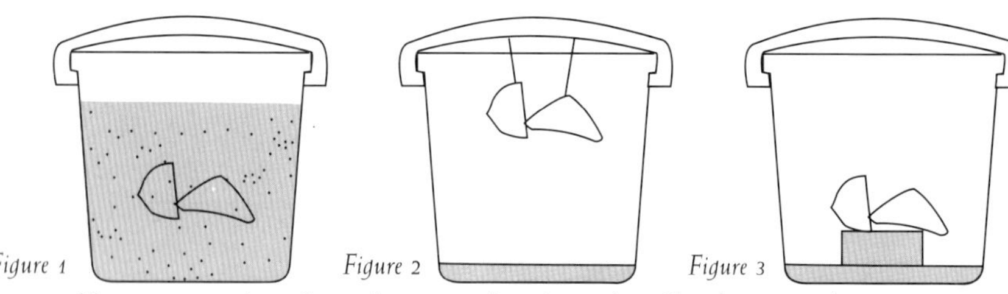

To create patina, bury the metal in saturated sawdust or litter (fig. 1), or suspend or set it over solution (figs. 2 and 3). Seal the container.

Liver of Sulfur

Liver of sulfur, mixed potassium sulphides, produces a range of grayish purple to black surface patinas, and an even broader color spectrum on copper. Available in a dry mix-it-yourself granular form or as a yellow liquid concentrate from crafts and metals suppliers, it smells bad but it's non-toxic. First, scrupulously clean the metal with copper and brass cleaner, ammonia, vinegar, or denatured alcohol. This process is particularly sensitive to oil or dirt, which will show up as undeveloped spots on the metal. Mix about ⅛ teaspoon (0.6 g) of dry material with 1 cup (0.24 L) of hot water, or follow the package directions to dilute the concentrate to a working solution, usually 1 tablespoon (15 mL) of concentrate to 1 cup (0.24 L) of the hottest water you can get from the tap. Use the working solution immediately. Leftover working solution lasts a week if sealed in an opaque container.

Try brushing on the solution with a paintbrush, sponging it on, or dipping your object in it. Some metals will turn black almost instantly. If you want to remove some of the black to create an antique effect, or to highlight relief work, wipe the solution off the high spots while it's still wet. It also will sand off easily after it has dried. The Bountiful Harvest Embossed Copper Journal on page 106 uses the wipe-off technique with beautiful results. Copper reacts to liver of sulfur with a gorgeous spectrum of colors and surface effects. Rinse the piece and don't touch the surface with your fingers until it's completly air-dried. If you don't like the result, sand it off and try again!

Preserving the Patina

Patinated metal pieces will continue to oxidize unless you seal them with a clear lacquer spray. The spray may cause copper pieces colored with liver of sulfur to lose the magenta spectrum of colors. Bright blues will recede, leaving you with warm oranges and reds, plus a little greenish blue. You'll have to decide whether to allow your piece to continue to change with exposure to air, or to fix the colors with sealer.

Patinas for Brass and Steel with Gun Bluing

Gun bluing, available at sporting goods stores, gives a patina to firearms, and it colors steel or brass with gray and black tones. Use a paintbrush to coat steel with the solution, or dip it into the solution. It can be applied to brass with steel wool. The reaction will occur immediately.

Rust

If you have an iron or steel piece that you want to "age" instantly, use a commercially made instant rust solution sold by craft suppliers. It reacts almost instantly. To slow it down, dilute it with water or alcohol starting with a one-to-one ratio, and add a tiny drop of dish soap to keep it from beading up on the surface of the metal. Try sponging it on for a more naturalistic, mottled effect.

Add-On Decorations

You can add beads, charms, and small found objects to metal projects, as shown in the Checkerboard Picture Frame on page 34. Glue them on, or drill holes and wire beads or trinkets through the metal. Solder dots and lines on metal also are attractive, but use a light hand. Try piercing holes with an awl, and glue in upholsterer's tacks, rivets, or studs. Install grommets with a grommet setter in metal mesh or thin sheet, as shown in the Greeting Card Gallery on page 102.

Protecting and Preserving Metal

Many of the metal projects in this book are finished with the application of sealer, most often a thin coat of clear acrylic spray. If you want to give a metal object some extra surface protection and it doesn't have delicate surface decoration that could be smeared or destroyed, you can also rub on a thin coating of paste furniture wax with a soft cloth. Warm the object first with a hair dryer or by placing it in a sunny spot, and it will be more receptive to the wax. Beeswax or paraffin are other traditional rub-on coatings. Clear nail polish seals small surfaces, and spray lacquer from art supply stores is useful for larger pieces.

Leonie Lacouette, Small Copper Pendulum, *1998, 12 x 6 x 3 in. (30.5 x 15.2 x 7.6 cm); particle board, copper, quartz pendulum movement; faux-finished, patinated. Photo by D. Egan*

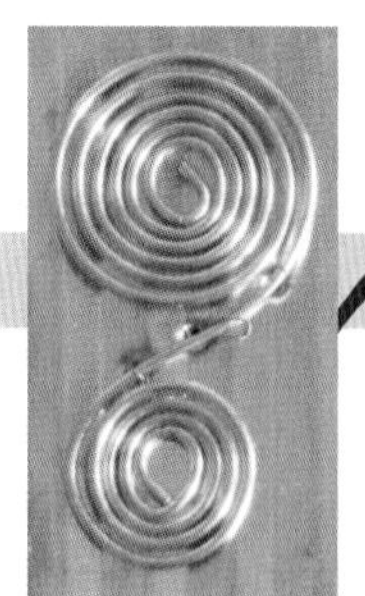

Home and Garden

Distressed Mirror Frame

Believe it or not, you'll use the same aluminum skirting that underpins mobile homes to create the frame for this stunning contemporary mirror. Easily applied acrylic paint creates its fashionable distressed look.

Materials

- Piece of aluminum skirting with a block pattern, 30 x 30 inches (76.2 x 76.2 cm)
- Acrylic craft paint in white, black, turquoise, ruby red metallic, and Venetian gold metallic
- Water-based, matte-finish, spray acrylic sealer
- Piece of plywood, 24 x 24 inches (61 x 61 cm)
- Mirror, 8 x 10 inches (20.3 x 25.4 cm)
- ⅜-inch (9.5 mm) short screws
- ⅜-inch (9.5 mm) common nails with heads
- Mirror mastic
- Old furnace grate or other found metal grid
- Picture hanger with attachment hardware

Tools and Supplies

- Steel wool
- Rag
- Foam brush
- Hammer
- Ruler
- Pencil
- Tin snips
- Electric drill with a small bit and a grinding bit
- Phillips head screwdriver

Instructions

1. Roughen the aluminum's surface with the steel wool. Wipe clean with the rag.

2. Use the foam brush to paint the aluminum, alternating and layering the colors. Wipe down the surface with the dampened rag between each coat, to give it a distressed look. Let dry and spray with the sealer.

3. Lay the painted aluminum on top of the plywood. Wrap the metal around the plywood, hammering the edges flat while folding them over like you make a bed. Peel back one edge of the aluminum and extract the plywood.

4. Position the mirror in the center of the aluminum, and measure the area where where it will sit. Draw around the mirror with the pencil.

5. Cut out a rectangular area in the metal with the tin snips to expose the mirror, but leave an extra margin of metal to overlap the mirror's edges. Smooth the edges with the sanding bit.

6. Slip the plywood back into its metal "sandwich." Fold and hammer down the open end again.

7. Use the Phillips head screwdriver to secure the wrapped metal to the back of the plywood with the ⅜-inch (9.5 mm) screws.

8. At the cutout in the metal, glue the mirror to the plywood using the mirror mastic. Let it dry for 24 hours.

9. Hammer the common nails around the cutout edge bordering the mirror.

10. Use the Phillips head screwdriver and a wood screw to attach the metal grate to the front of the mirror.

11. Attach the picture hanger to the back of the frame.

Designer,
Jean Tomaso Moore

Woven Copper Coasters

These handsome coasters are a simple but stunning use of glass, foil tape, and bits of copper.

Designer, *Travis Waldron*

MATERIALS

- 8 pieces of single-strength glass, 4 x 4 inches (10.2 x 10.2 cm) each
- 8 strips of 36-gauge copper tooling foil, 12 x ½ inches (30.5 x 30.5 cm) each
- 3 yards (2.7 m) of ½-inch (1.3 cm) copper foil tape, with adhesive back

TOOLS AND SUPPLIES

- Glass cleaner
- Paper towel
- Needle-nose pliers
- Tin snips
- Candle
- Matches or lighter
- Burnishing tool

INSTRUCTIONS

1. Clean both sides of the glass pieces with the glass cleaner and paper towel, and set them aside in a clean, dry place.

2. Light the candle. Holding one 12-inch (30.5 cm) copper strip with the needle-nose pliers grasping its middle, slowly pass the entire length of the strip over the candle flame to make attractive, lasting color changes in the copper. Any soot that forms underneath will be cleaned off later.

3. Heat three more strips using the same technique.

4. Clean any soot off the strips with glass cleaner and a paper towel.

5. You now have four strips of intentionally tarnished copper and four strips of plain copper. With the tin snips, cut all the strips into pieces about 3 inches (7.6 cm) long, but don't be too exact; when you weave the pieces, uneven edges will be desirable.

6. Now you're ready to weave together four plain and four tarnished pieces of copper for each coaster. Place four pieces side by side, alternating the plain and tarnished pieces, and do a simple over-and-under weave of the four remaining pieces, also alternating plain and tarnished. Repeat until you've woven a total of four coasters.

7. Hold the edges with your fingertips, and place one piece of glass on your work surface. Make sure the glass is print- and dust-free. Place a woven piece in the center and "sandwich" it with a second piece of glass. Check again for position and any dust that needs removing.

8. Cut four 4⅛-inch (10.5 cm) pieces of copper foil tape. Peel ¼ inch (6 mm) of the backing off the back of one strip, exposing the adhesive. Set aside.

9. Carefully lift the "sandwich," maintaining steady pressure on both pieces of glass to keep the woven copper from shifting. Adhere the exposed adhesive end of the foil tape to the corner of the sandwich, centering it over the two pieces of glass. Slowly peel away the rest of the tape backing while adhering the tape to the entire length of the side of the glass. Trim any excess with the scissors.

10. You'll note that the tape is wider than the edge of the sandwich. Fold down the extra tape on both sides of the sandwich, pressing it firmly to adhere it to the glass and complete the seal.

11. Apply another piece of foil tape to the opposite side of the sandwich in the same manner, then repeat the process on the two remaining sides.

12. Construct and seal the three remaining coasters.

13. Use the burnishing tool to firmly and repeatedly rub the foil on all four sides and edges of each coaster to ensure a good bond, then clean the outside with glass cleaner.

Checkerboard Picture Frame

Woven strips of foil combine with wire accents to turn this readymade frame into the picture of fun! Off-the-shelf beads and tiny bells add to its whimsy.

Designer, *Kathleen M. Anderson*

MATERIALS

- 2 sheets of lightweight copper foil, each 9¼ x 12 inches (23.5 cm)
- 2 sheets of lightweight aluminum foil, each 9¼ x 12 inches (23.5 cm)
- Wooden picture frame, 11 x 12½ inches (28 x 32 cm) with 5 x 7-inch (12.7 x 17.8 cm) image opening
- Lightweight copper mesh, 16 x 20 inches (40.5 x 51 cm) with ⅛-inch (3 mm) weave
- Photograph of your choice
- Piece of brown paper, 11 x 12½ inches (28 x 32 cm)
- Piece of felt, same size as picture frame
- Spool of 16-gauge bare copper wire
- Spool of 32-gauge tinned copper wire
- Assorted beads and bells
- Picture hanger with attachment hardware

TOOLS AND SUPPLIES

- Scissors
- Thumb tacks
- Craft glue
- 12-inch (30.5 cm) rolling pin or brayer
- Wax paper
- Books or other weights
- Needle-nose pliers
- Sewing needle
- Wire cutter

INSTRUCTIONS

1. Use the scissors to cut six copper foil strips measuring 1⅛ x 12 inches (2.8 x 30.5 cm), eight strips measuring 1⅛ x 6½ inches (2.8 x 16.5 cm), and six strips measuring 1⅛ x 4 inches (2.8 x 10.2 cm). Save the scrap.

2. Cut six 1⅛ x 12-inch (2.8 x 30.5 cm) aluminum foil strips and 12 strips measuring 1⅛ x 6½ inches (2.8 x 16.5 cm). Save the scrap.

3. Tack six of the 1⅛ x 12-inch (2.8 x 30.5 cm) copper strips along the 11-inch (28 cm) frame back, using three strips behind the top right-hand corner and three behind the top left-hand corner. Drape the ends over the front.

4. Tack four 1⅛ x 6½-inch (2.8 x 16.5 cm) strips above the frame's inner opening and four below. Weave the six 1⅛ x 12-inch (2.8 x 30.5 cm) aluminum strips side to side, across the top and bottom of the front and through the copper strips. Tack in back.

5. Place six 1⅛ x 6½ inch (2.8 x 16.5 cm) aluminum strips to the left and six to the right of the opening. Weave them. Tack the loose ends to the back, and push the other ends into the frame's photo indention. The whole frame should be covered with strips, and all strips tacked to the back. The horizontal aluminum strips will be glued later.

6. Add six 1⅛ x 4-inch (2.8 x 10.2 cm) copper strips to extend the copper strips down the front. Slip them in place under the woven pieces and tack to the back.

7. Remove the tacks one by one, gluing the strips to the back. Glue the horizontal aluminum strips to the frame sides.

8. Cut ¾-inch-wide (1.9 cm) strips from the scraps, and use them to cover the edges of the frame. Tack down.

9. Open the mesh, and roll away folds with the rolling pin or brayer. Center the mesh over the frame, and use the scissors to cut an X over its opening. Bring the cut edges to the back, pushing them into the photo slot and tacking in back. Use the mesh to wrap the frame like a package, and tack the mesh down.

10. Slip your photo into the frame, and glue the brown paper on the back. Lay the frame face up on the wax paper, place the felt on top, and use the books or other heavy objects to weight it down so the felt holds the mesh firmly to the frame. Leave overnight.

11. Remove the felt. With the needle-nose pliers, make differently sized coils of the 16-gauge wire. Use the needle and 32-gauge wire to sew them on in random spots. Leave a tail of wire, and thread it through the beads and bells. Knot the wire and clip the end with the wire cutters.

12. Attach the picture hanger.

Fusion Clock

What does it take to create the elegant bends and curves of this two-tone clock? Only careful cutting and the simplest of tools. It's easy.

Designers, *Doug Hays and Penny Cash*

Materials

- Clock face templates (see page 134)
- Piece of copper roofing flashing, 12 x 12 inches (30.5 x 30.5 cm)*
- Piece of aluminum roofing flashing, 12 x 12 inches (30.5 x 30.5 cm)*
- Sheet of ¼-inch-thick (6 mm) foam core board, 5 x 5 inches (12.7 x 12.7 cm)
- 4 #10 machine screws, ¾ inch (1.9 cm) long
- 4 #10 knurled nuts
- 4 #10 cap nuts
- Clock motor including a shaft with ⅞-inch (2.2 cm) minimum length
- Clock hands
- Battery for clock motor
- Short length of water line copper tubing (optional)

  *Available from a roofing or gutter supplier

Tools and Supplies

- Scissors
- Scribe
- Tin snips or aviation shears
- Half-round fine file
- Electric drill, preferably variable speed
- Mounted 1-inch grinding stone for the drill
- Drill bits to match the machine screws and clock motor shaft
- Small ball-peen hammer
- Masking tape
- Needle-nose pliers
- 2 small C-clamps or pony clamps
- 2 small pieces of cardboard
- Fine-tip permanent marker
- Ruler
- Craft knife

INSTRUCTIONS

1. Use a photocopier to enlarge the larger of the two clock face templates so it fits an 8½ x 11-inch (21.6 x 28 cm) sheet of paper. Enlarge the second template, keeping it proportionately smaller relative to the first template. Cut out the first template with the scissors.

2. Use the scribe to outline the larger template on the copper.

3. Carefully cut out the pattern with the snips or shears.

4. Shape and clean up the edges with the file and the drill with the grinding stone attached. Gently flatten the edges with the hammer.

5. Repeat steps 2 through 4 with the smaller template and the aluminum flashing. Keep the paper template.

6. Mark the holes for the bolts and the clock motor shaft by taping the template to the aluminum and forcefully scribing the positions through the paper.

7. By hand, gently bend down the sections on the copper piece marked "O." Use a series of small bends rather than bending all at once, or the metal will crease and lose its gracefulness.

8. Barely curl the tips back and upward with the needle-nose pliers.

9. Curl the tabs marked "X" inward with the pliers. Grab a small section of the end with the long edge of the pliers (fig. 1) and with a twisting motion, wrap the copper around the shape of the pliers (see figs. 2 and 3).

10. Curl and bend the aluminum the same way, but reverse the direction of the curl of the "X'd" corner sections.

11. Lay the aluminum on top of the copper and center it. Use the two C-clamps to hold them in place, with a small piece of cardboard under each clamp to protect the aluminum.

12. Drill a hole at the 12, three, six, and nine o' clock positions for the machine screws, and drill the center hole for the clock motor shaft.

13. Place the aluminum on the foam core, and mark the four number positions on the foam core with the pen. Remove the aluminum.

14. Connect the dots on the foam core using the fine-tip permanent marker and the ruler to make a diamond shape. Cut along the lines with the craft knife, and cut about ⅛ inch (3 mm) off each point. The foam core will create a space between the two metal faces. Bolt the two pieces together with the machine screws and the knurled nuts. Tighten lightly, and add the cap nuts.

15. Install the clock motor, hands, and hanger according to the manufacturer's instructions. Because the shaft has to be long enough to let the hands clear the cap nuts, you can cover the threads with the short length of water line copper tubing if you wish.

16. Make sure the hands can make a full circle and clear the tops of the cap nuts.

17. Set the clock and install the battery.

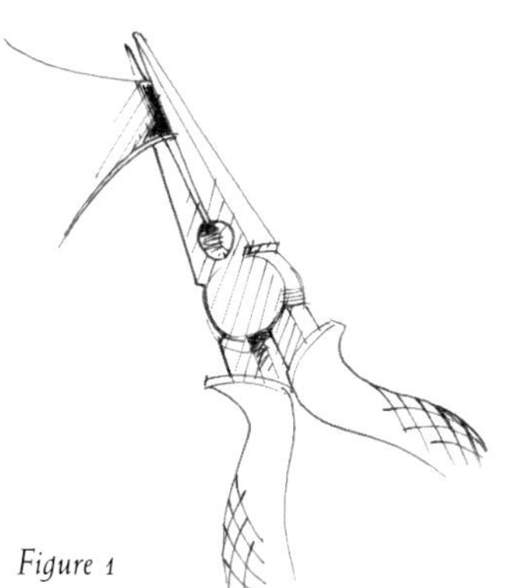

Figure 1

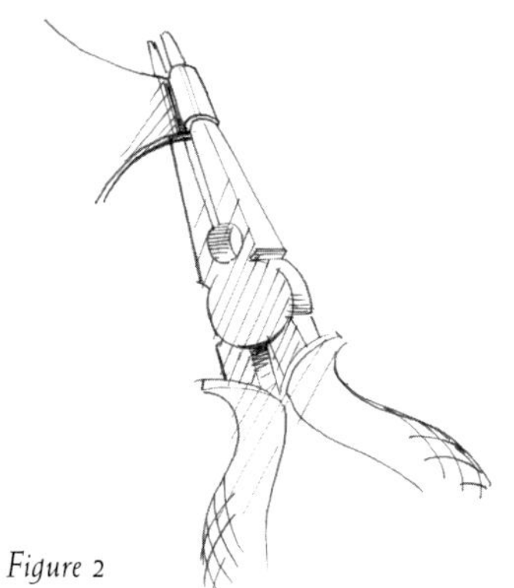

Figure 2

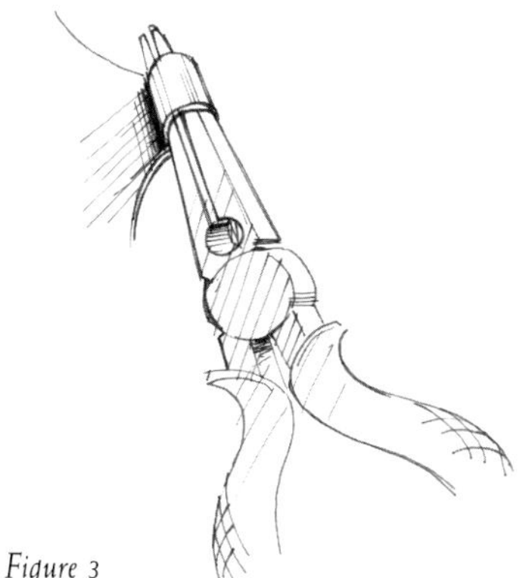

Figure 3

Cosmic Copper Relief Tabletop

The heavenly bodies in this inventive tabletop are easily hammered into copper sheet using ready-made materials like PVC pipe cap to create the imagery. The top was created to fit a base that came from a flea market.

Designer, *Ivan Bailey*

MATERIALS

- Table base (the example shown is 18 inches [45.7 cm] square)
- Piece of 16-ounce (448 g) copper roof flashing*
- 1 PVC pipe cap, paint can, coffee can, or steel ring, 10 inches (25.4 cm) in diameter
- 1 smaller PVC pipe cap, pipe, or other circular object
- Piece 3/16-inch (4.8 mm) welding rod, not coated with flux, 18 inches (45.7 cm) long*
- Piece of 3/4-inch (1.9 cm) round, plain mild steel, 6 inches (15.2 cm) long*
- Paste wax

*Flashing is available from a roofing or gutter supplier. Welding rod and steel bar are sold by industrial metals distributors.

TOOLS AND SUPPLIES

- Tape measure
- Grease pencil
- Piece of wooden board
- Metal shears
- Fine sandpaper
- Ball-peen hammer
- Medium-size hammer with wooden handle
- Electric sander
- Hacksaw
- Cross-peen hammer or other large, flat-faced hammer
- Trailer hitch ball or other heavy, spherical, solid metal object
- Wooden board
- Right angle grinder
- Flat file
- Triangular file
- Light sledgehammer or stonemason's hammer
- Nails or screws, for attaching to tabletop (optional)
- Scouring pad
- Small handheld propane torch
- Matches or lighter
- Rag

INSTRUCTIONS

1. Measure your tabletop, and add 1/2 inch (1.3 cm) to the length and 1/2 inch (1.3 cm) to the width to allow for a 1/4-inch (6 mm) overhang on all sides.

2. Using the pencil, draw the dimensions on the copper sheet, and cut along the outside of the outline with the metal shears. Using the sandpaper, lightly sand the edges.

3. To make the moon, place the 10-inch (25.4 cm) diameter PVC pipe cap, can, or other circular object on the underside of the copper piece. Hold the piece of copper firmly against the cap or can, grasping the copper at the point furthest away from the hammer. Make several decisive blows with the ball-peen hammer to define the inner edges of the ring and to form what's called a "dish bulge." Use the PVC pipe cap or coffee can, ball-peen hammer, and same technique to make the Earth.

4. To create the moon craters, turn the copper right side up, and dimple the craters using the smaller piece of PVC and ball-peen hammer.

5. Now you'll create a relief tool to form the Earth's swirly cloud lines. Use the electric sander to sand down the end of the medium-weight hammer handle to a roundish knob, and cut a small V-shaped trench in it with the hacksaw. Hammer the tool on the copper with the cross-peen hammer.

6. To create the planished (slightly dimpled) effect on the entire copper surface, strike the trailer hitch ball against the copper with the flat face of the ball-peen hammer.

7. To make the curved lines representing planetary dust rings, use the 3/16-inch (4.8 mm) welding rod. Bend the rod to the curve you want, and cut it into various lengths with the hacksaw. Lay the copper on the wooden board, position a piece of rod on top, and strike it with the heavy hammer. Discard the rod after a couple of blows in the same spot because it will deform and won't lie flat.

8. Make the star stamp from the 6-inch (15.2 cm) length of 3/4-inch (1.9 cm) steel. Rough out the star shape from the steel with the right-angle grinder, and finish the inner corners of the star with the flat and triangular files. Place the star stamp on the copper's right side, and hit it with the light sledgehammer or stonemason's hammer.

9. If the copper relief will sit inside the open top of the table base, position the edge of the copper so it hangs over the wooden board about 1/4 inch (6 mm), and carefully hammer the copper to a 90° angle. Do this on all four sides. Drop the top into the framework. You also can size the top to cover the existing surface of a table, then nail or screw it into place.

10. Scour the surface with the scouring pad, then use the propane torch to make some color accents in the copper.

11. With the rag, rub a thin film of the paste wax on the copper to protect the metal.

Days-Gone-By Embossed Frame

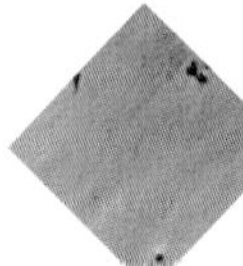

Gentle strands of wheat in a design complemented by embossed brass and rich copper give this lovely frame an old-time feel.

Designer, *Dolores Ruzicka*

MATERIALS

- Brass tooling foil, 10 x 12 inches (25.4 x 30.5 cm)
- Wheat border pattern (see page 134)
- Black acrylic paint
- Clear acrylic, matte finish spray sealer
- Copper tooling foil, 7 x 9 inches (17.8 x 23 cm)
- 2 pieces of adhesive-backed board, each 8 x 10 inches (20.3 x 25.4 cm)
- 1 piece of adhesive-backed board, 5 x 7 inches (12.7 x 17.8 cm)
- Liver of sulfur*
- Sawtooth picture hanger

*available from crafts, jewelry, and metal suppliers

TOOLS AND SUPPLIES

- Pad of newspapers, ½ inch (1.3 cm) thick
- Masking tape
- Stylus
- Paintbrush, ½ inch (1.3 cm) wide
- Steel wool
- Scissors
- Tacky glue

INSTRUCTIONS

1. Use a photocopier to enlarge the template so the wheat pattern is approximately 10 inches (25 cm) long. Lay the brass tooling foil onto the pad of newspapers, and position the pattern on the foil. Tape the pattern in place with the masking tape.

2. Trace the pattern onto the brass with the stylus. Remove the pattern and retrace the design with the stylus to deepen the lines. Make random dots with the stylus on the background of the brass.

3. Apply the black acrylic paint to the brass with the paintbrush, and let it dry.

4. Buff off the black paint with the steel wool, leaving paint in the embossed design. Spray the entire surface with the clear sealer.

5. Peel off the protective paper from the 8 x 10-inch (20.3 x 25.4 cm) piece of the adhesive board. Position the brass on the adhesive side, and fold the overlap of the brass to the back of the board. Remove the paper from the other 8 x 10-inch (20.3 x 25.4 cm) piece of adhesive-backed board, and attach it to the backside of the brass piece to give the back a finished appearance.

6. Peel off the protective paper on the 5 x 7-inch (12.7 x 17.8 cm) adhesive frame. Position the copper tooling foil on the adhesive, and use the scissors to score and remove the section of copper in the center of the frame.

7. Fold the tabs of copper to the backside of the frame. Place the copper onto the newspaper pad, and use the stylus to make lines about ⅛ inch (3 mm) apart as shown.

8. Following the package directions, use the paintbrush to apply the liver of sulfur to the copper. The metal will turn black. With the steel wool, buff off the excess black to achieve a rich, aged effect.

9. With the scissors, cut several ¼-inch-wide (6 mm) strips of adhesive backing, and use them to adhere the copper frame to the brass background, positioning the photograph of your choice under the frame.

Phases of the Moon Pendulum Clock

Past, present, and future phases of the moon glint invitingly from this clever clock. The design combines the old and the new, featuring a "found" metal gear and extra lunar accents. Adapt the instructions to fit your own special objects.

Designer, *Jean Tomaso Moore*

MATERIALS

- Sheet of rusty metal, 8 x 10 inches (20.3 x 25.4 cm)
- Acrylic craft paint in black, ruby-red metallic, bronze and/or copper metallic colors
- Rubber stamp with a large spiral design
- Spool of 18- or 20-gauge wire, rust-colored
- Rusty metal gear, 12 inches (30.5 cm) in diameter
- Piece of aluminum flashing, 7 x 22 inches (17.8 x 56 cm)
- Rubber stamp with a sun or antique face design
- Stamp ink
- Paper
- Water-based, matte-finish, spray acrylic sealer
- 3 crescent moon charms
- 5 distressed metal beads or other small objects
- Rusty, distressed metal pieces, found objects, and jewelry parts
- Battery-powered pendulum clock movement
- 1 star cut out of rusty metal

TOOLS AND SUPPLIES

- Tin snips or metal shears
- C-clamps or table vise
- Electric drill and drill bits
- Wire cutters
- Needle-nose pliers
- Industrial-strength adhesive
- Hammer
- Small plastic cup
- Paintbrush
- Scissors
- White craft glue
- Double-faced tape
- Ruler

INSTRUCTIONS

1. Use the tin snips or shears to cut a disk 3½ inches (8.9 cm) in diameter from the rusty sheet metal for the clock face in the center of the gear. Secure the disk to the work surface with a C-clamp or vise, and drill a hole through the center of the disk to accommodate the shaft that controls the clock hands.

2. Brush a light coat of bronze acrylic paint on the spiral-design rubber stamp. Press the design onto the center of the metal clock-face disk.

3. Use the wire cutters to cut four 2-inch (5 cm) pieces of rust-colored wire. Twist each piece with the needle-nose pliers into a tight spiral. Glue the spirals to the clock face with the industrial-strength adhesive, positioning them at three, six, nine and 12 o'clock.

4. Place the clock face over the center hole of the rusty gear, and glue it in place with the industrial-strength adhesive.

5. Use the snips to cut two 1½-inch (3.8 cm) equilateral triangles from the sheet metal. Drill two holes ¼ inch (6 mm) apart in the center of each triangle. Place the triangles over the small holes on the adjacent sides of the gear. To create the clock's hanger in back, thread a continuous length of the wire back and forth through the holes in the triangles, and back again through the gear holes.

6. Cut three circular disks, 2½ inches (6.4 cm) in diameter, from the aluminum flashing. The disks will cover holes in the gear. Using the hammer, tap each disk over its respective hole to create a curved and distressed surface.

7. Mix the metallic and black paints together in the plastic cup. Paint the surface of each hammered aluminum disk, striving for an "aged" patina.

8. Cover the rubber sun-face stamp with stamp ink and make three impressions on a piece of paper. Use a photocopier to enlarge the faces if necessary to obtain 2-inch (5 cm) diameters. Then cut them out with the scissors.

9. Brush a wash of copper or bronze paint over the paper faces for an "aged" look. Let them dry. Use the white craft glue to glue each face to the circles of flashing you've already cut, hammered and painted. When gluing, position the faces in "moon phase" fashion: the left face half coming into view, the center face shown in full, and the right face half moving out of the circle. When they're dry, spray the disks with a thin layer of clear acrylic sealer.

10. Cut two circles 1½ inches (3.8 cm) in diameter from the rusty sheet metal, and glue them with industrial-strength adhesive to the back of other openings in the gear. Add the crescent moon charms in different positions inside the circles, gluing them in place with industrial-strength adhesive.

11. Attach the beads and decorative objects by threading wire through each bead and running it through smaller holes in the gear to the back side of the clock. Twist the wire ends with the needle-nose pliers to secure. Attach the other found objects with the adhesive or wire.

12. Use the double-faced tape to attach the plastic clock mechanism to the back of the gear. Assemble the clock and add the hands.

13. Design the pendulum facade to be attached to the rod mechanism, and mark the design on the aluminum flashing. Then cut it out with the tin snips. For the clock shown, a pendulum 1½ inches (3.8 cm) wide balanced out the weighty clock body.

(continued on page 44)

Pendulum Clock, *continued*

14. Paint the pendulum cutout with a mixture of the paint colors to blend with the rest of the clock. Allow to dry.

15. Drill holes in the top and bottom of the facade and in the existing pendulum rod. Drill holes through the rusty metal star.

16. Attach the facade to the pendulum rod by cutting small pieces of wire with the wire cutters, threading the wires through the holes you've drilled in the facade and rod, and twisting them securely. Attach the star at the bottom of the pendulum to serve as its bob. Hook the pendulum to the clock mechanism.

17. Hang the clock, making sure it's level so the pendulum swings freely.

Kitchenware Angel

This friendly angel wears her heart on her sleeve, and her curls are to die for! A spiral wire hanger helps you hang her up to watch benignly over your home.

Materials

- Roll of 16-gauge galvanized steel wire
- 2 metal tablespoons
- Piece of wire mesh, 8 x 20 inches (20.3 x 50.8 cm)
- Roll of 26-gauge brass wire
- 24 inches (61 cm) of wire-edged ribbon, 2½ inches wide (6.4 cm)
- 2 steel wool pot scrubber pads
- Piece of aluminum flashing, ½ x ½ inches square (1.3 x 1.3 cm)

Tools and Supplies

- Wire cutters
- Needle-nose pliers
- Dull pencil or stylus
- Utility scissors
- Awl or ice pick

Instructions

1. Cut a 34-inch (86.4 cm) length of steel wire with the wire cutters. With the needle-nose pliers, wrap one end tightly around the spoon at the point where the handle meets the bowl. Twist the other end of the wire into a 1-inch (2.5 cm) decorative spiral by gripping the wire end with the pliers while turning the wire, using your other hand to help guide the wire as you turn it. Form a large C-shaped hook after the spiral, and bend the rest of the wire in a zigzag.

2. Turn the spoon so the domed side faces up. Cut an 8-inch (20.3 cm) piece of steel wire for the arms. Make a slight bend in the center, position the bend at the base of the bowl, and wrap the ends around the spoon. Make ½-inch (1.3 cm) spirals on the ends with the pliers. Curve the arms toward the center front.

3. With the scissors, carefully cut a 6 x 16-inch (15.2 x 40.6 cm) piece of mesh for the dress and a 4 x 8-inch (10.2 x 20.3 cm) piece for the wings. On one 16-inch (40.6 cm) edge of the dress and all around the wings, create hems by folding up ⅛ inch (3 mm) and rubbing it with the second spoon. Join the two 6-inch (15.2 cm) ends the same way.

4. Put the spoon handle in the dress, bringing the dress just under the arm wires, hemmed end reaching the tabletop. Press the top edge of the dress together, and wrap it tightly in place around the spoon with the brass wire.

5. Pinch the 8-inch (20.3 cm) sides of the wings together in the center. Cut a 14-inch (35.6 cm) length of the brass wire, and wrap it twice around the wings' center. Center the wings at the top of the dress behind the angel. Secure with more wraps of the brass wire.

6. Tie the wire-edged ribbon around the spoon in a bow under the angel's chin.

7. Slightly pull the strands of the steel wool scrubbing pads apart and place the "hair" over the spoon bowl, wrapping it around the wire hanger and the spoon's sides.

8. With the pencil or stylus, trace a heart shape on the aluminum flashing. Cut it out and poke a hole in the top with the awl or ice pick. Cut a 16-inch (40.6 cm) length of brass wire, fold it in half, and twist it slightly to make a double wire strand. Thread the heart onto one end. Curl the wire by wrapping it loosely around a pencil, and wrap the free end of the wire through the spiral ends of the arms.

Designer, *Barbara Matthiessen*

Soda Can Picture Frame

This fun project is a terrific way to reuse empty aluminum drink cans by wrapping them around a ready-made frame or stretcher. Select a variety of cans to take advantage of their bright colors and bold grapics.

Designer, *Neil Benson*

MATERIALS

- Aluminum drink cans
- Wooden picture frame or canvas stretcher*
- 8 thin wood slats, slightly shorter and narrower than the frame
- Sawtooth picture hanger with attachment hardware
- Piece of backing board cut to fit the image area
- Piece of glass cut to fit the image area

  *available from an art supply store

TOOLS AND SUPPLIES

- Safety can opener
- Metal shears
- Guillotine-style paper cutter
- Staple gun with ¼-inch (6 mm) staples
- Hammer
- 2 wood screws, long enough to connect the depth of two slats plus the frame
- Newspapers

INSTRUCTIONS

1. With the safety can opener, cut along the side of each can and remove its top and rim. Cut down to the bottom with shears, then cut off the bottom. Trim the can to a rectangle with the paper cutter or shears. Prepare enough cans to cover the frame.

2. To cover the frame, use a folding technique on the corners similar to gift wrapping. Center a flattened can on the corner at a 45° angle and hold it down.

3. Cut from the outside in to the wood with the shears, along a line parallel to an edge of the frame.

4. Fold both sides of the cut metal down against the frame sides. Fold the extra-long side of the can to a 90° angle, and slip it under the metal that's flush with the corner.

5. From the back of the frame, cut a slot in the metal at the outside of the corner so that two pieces can be folded flat against the back of the frame. Crease the folded edges neatly and staple the corner pocket of metal against the wood. Trim off any metal outside the staples.

6. Cut the stapled can from the inside to the wood, along the arms of an imaginary X crossing the frame. Bend both cut sides to the back, and fit a small L-shaped piece of can inside the corner of the frame to cover the bare spot. Fold back the two sides and staple everything in place.

7. Finish all four corners. Cover the front by overlapping, bending, and stapling the cans.

8. Place the frame facedown on the newspaper, and hammer the staples flat against the back.

9. Make a holding slot for the photograph, backing, and glass. Staple three slatwood strips onto the frame back, their edges close to the frame's outside edges. Staple three more slats on top, their edges close to the inside of the frame. Staple the last two pieces together. Slip the glass, photo, and backing board in place. Use the wood screws to screw the bottom pieces over one end to hold everything in place.

10. Attach the sawtooth picture hanger.

Perk-Up Coffee Cup Napkin Rings

Food shopping can be a treasure hunt if you keep an eye peeled for cans to use in metal projects. The imagery shown on these napkin rings came from a Latino-brand coffee can.

Designer, *Terry Taylor*

Materials

- 4 small, smooth-sided cans, such as evaporated milk cans
- Cans with images you'd like to use
- Aluminum pop rivets

Tools and Supplies

- Safety can opener
- Half-round or flat file
- Scouring pad
- Wire cutter
- Tin snips or metal shears
- Masking tape
- Hole punch for metal
- Awl
- Fine-tip permanent marker
- Pop-rivet gun

Instructions

1. Using the can opener, remove the top and bottom from one of the four cans. Wash and dry the can.

2. Use the file to smooth any jagged edges from the interior of the can, then use the scouring pad to remove any burrs. Set aside.

3. Working with the tin you've chosen for its imagery, remove its top and bottom with the can opener. Use the wire cutter to make several nips in the wire edge around the can, and make a couple of nips at the top and bottom edges at the seam. Don't use the tin snips to do this as it will ruin them.

4. Cut down the seam line of the tin with the snips or shears, and remove any wire edge if necessary.

5. Cut out the images as desired from the opened tin, and trim them to your satisfaction. Use a scouring pad to smooth any rough edges, and set the cutouts aside.

6. Place the image on a clean can. You may have to bend the image slightly to conform to the can.

7. Use the hole punch or awl to make a hole in the top and bottom of the cutout image. Place the image back on the can, and mark the can at both points with the awl or marker.

8. Remove the image and make holes with the punch at the marks you've made on the can. Use the pop rivets and pop-rivet gun to fasten the image to the can. Make the other three napkin rings.

Garden Party Planters

With a little solder and a hand-held propane torch, you can turn thrift store serving dishes into tall outdoor containers. Fill them with bird seed or bright flowers, then sit back and join the party!

Designer, *Tamara Miller*

MATERIALS

- Silver-plated trays, bowls, coffeepot, or teapot
- Copper pipe, ¾-inch (1.9 cm) inner diameter, in desired lengths
- ¼-inch (6 mm) threaded rod, in lengths to match the copper pipe
- Bird seed or flowers

TOOLS AND SUPPLIES

- Tape measure
- Fine-tip permanent marker
- Pipe cutter
- Electric drill with ¼-inch (6 mm) drill bit
- Hacksaw
- ¼-inch (6 mm) nuts and washers
- Denatured alcohol
- Rag
- Lead-free solder
- Flux
- Short-bristled brush
- Propane hand torch
- Fine sandpaper

INSTRUCTIONS

1. Choose your trays or pots, and decide how tall their supporting pipes will be. Keep them low enough to reach the top for bird seed refills or watering flowers. A group also looks best if the heights are varied.

2. Measure the pipe lengths you want. Mark them with the marker, and cut the pipe with the pipe cutter.

3. With the electric drill and ¼-inch (6 mm) bit, drill a hole in the center of the trays and through the bottoms of the pots. Secure the trays or pots with a vise before drilling to keep them stationary.

4. Measure the thickness of the tray or height of the pot, and add that amount to the length of its supporting copper pipe. Measure a length of threaded rod to match the total. The rod should be long enough to extend from the top of the tray or pot through its bottom and through to the opposite end of the copper pipe. Cut the rod with the hacksaw.

5. Screw one end of the threaded rod through the tray or pot, and secure it on top with a nut and washer. Run the other end of the rod through its copper pipe "sleeve."

6. Now solder the serving piece and the copper pipe. At the points where they're to be soldered, clean both surfaces with the rag saturated with denatured alcohol to remove any dirt and oil from the metals. Working in a well-ventilated area, use the brush to apply the flux at the join of the tray and the copper pipe, then solder. See page 23 for more information on soldering.

7. Sand the copper pipe lightly with the sandpaper. The copper will acquire a rich patina from exposure to outdoor elements.

8. Fill the vessels with bird seed or flowers.

Dragonfly Plaque

Now you can capture a creature as elusive as a dragonfly to enjoy all year round. The use of four different metals and a simple copper patina technique gives extra visual interest to this handsome plaque.

Designer, *Barbara Matthiessen*

MATERIALS

- Piece of lightweight tin sheeting, 12 x 15 inches (30.5 x 38 cm)
- Salt
- Water
- Tracing paper
- Dragonfly template (see page 135)
- Piece of lightweight aluminum flashing, 8 x 10 inches (20.3 x 25.4 cm)
- Piece of lightweight copper sheeting, 9 x 12 inches (23 x 30.5 cm)
- 4 pop rivets, ¼-inch (6 mm)
- 12-inch (30.5 cm) brass bead chain with two connectors

TOOLS AND SUPPLIES

- Sheet of plastic or newspapers
- Tin snips
- Sandpaper, medium-grade
- Pencil
- Masking tape
- Scissors
- Stylus
- Pop-rivet gun
- Power drill with a drill bit sized to match the chain bead
- Industrial-strength adhesive

INSTRUCTIONS

1. Cut the metal sheeting to size with the tin snips if necessary.

2. Put the copper on the plastic or newspapers, and "age" it by dampening the metal with water and sprinkling on the salt. For the next two days, add more of both until the patina reaches the desired intensity.

3. Sand the tin with a swirling motion to create a brushed appearance.

4. Trace the dragonfly template with pencil and paper, and tape it to the aluminum sheet. Trace over all the lines with the pencil or stylus, and make dots in the eye areas.

5. Use the scissors to cut the dragonfly out of the aluminum. Turn it over to expose its back side, and heavily emboss the lines on the body by rubbing with the pencil or stylus in a wide band.

6. Center the copper on top of the tin, and fasten with a pop-rivet in each corner.

7. On a 12-inch (30.5 cm) side of the tin, drill holes in the two corners for the brass bead chain hanger. Thread the chain through the front of the drilled holes, and snap a connector onto each end of the chain to secure.

8. Apply the adhesive to the back of the dragonfly, and adhere it to the copper sheet. Allow to dry before hanging.

VERDIGRIS FISH MOBILE

A beautiful rust and blue-green patina is easy to create on the cut-out copper. All it takes is a plastic bag, ammonia, and kitty litter!

Designer, *Margaret Dahm*

MATERIALS

- Fish templates (see page 134)
- Piece of tracing or copier paper
- Small piece of 16-ounce (448 g) sheet copper
- Galvanized steel wire, 14 to 16-gauge
- Copper tubing, ¼-inch (6 mm) diameter
- 1 cup (.24 L) of ammonia
- 1 quart (.95 L) of cat litter
- Plastic bag

TOOLS AND SUPPLIES

- Fine-tip permanent marker
- Scissors
- Tin snips
- Regular pliers
- Piece of wood
- Nail, with diameter larger than the steel wire
- Hammer
- Needle-nose pliers
- Wire cutters
- Rubber gloves

INSTRUCTIONS

1. Trace the head and tail templates with the marker and paper, enlarging them if desired, and cut them out with the scissors. Trace them onto the copper sheet, and use the tin snips to cut out the two pieces. Cut just outside the tracing lines, except for the tail; leave a ¼-inch (6 mm) margin around it.

2. Make ¼-inch long (6 mm) cuts with the snips around the perimeter of the tail, with ½-inch (1.3 cm) between each cut. Use the regular pliers to bend these pieces so they're perpendicular to the tail. Set aside.

3. Place the head on the wood. Use the nail and hammer to punch two holes in the flat edge, spacing them to divide the edge into quarters.

4. Use the needle-nose pliers to roughly measure the distance between the two punched holes. Bend the end of the wire the same length and at a slight angle; insert it into a hole in the fish head and through the next hole. Bend the angle up on the opposite side and back to the original entry point.

5. Bend the wire to form a loose, flattened spiral of fish "ribs." When the rib section is long enough, bend the wire into and around the tail piece, inside its upturned edges. Clip the wire with the wire cutters.

6. Bend in the tail's upturned edges using the needle-nose pliers, and hammer the bent edges flat to join the tail to the body.

7. Flatten 2 inches (5 cm) at the end of the copper tubing with the hammer, and bend a small U-turn in the end with the needle-nose pliers. Holding the U at the top, bend the flat tubing straight down, then crimp it up about ¼ inch (6 mm). The rest of the tube will form a gentle arc under which the fish will hang.

8. Cut a 4-inch (10.2 cm) piece of wire and make a loop around the top of the second fish rib. Loop the other end of the wire around the crimped end of the tubing, and check that the fish dangles roughly at the center of the arc. Loop the wire tightly at the bottom of the crimped end of tubing to secure it. Adjust the tubing arc and cut the end with the snips.

9. Wearing the rubber gloves, mix the ammonia and cat litter in a plastic bag and bury the mobile in the mixture. Don't breathe the fumes. Close the bag, and let the piece sit for a few days to develop a patina. If there are any spots lacking rust or verdigris after this time, rebury the piece in the mixture and process it for a few more days.

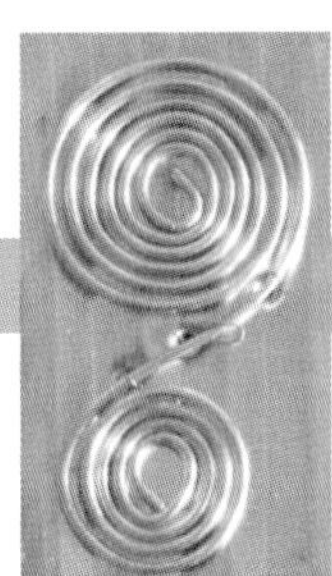

The Lighting Department

Rustic Moose Lamp

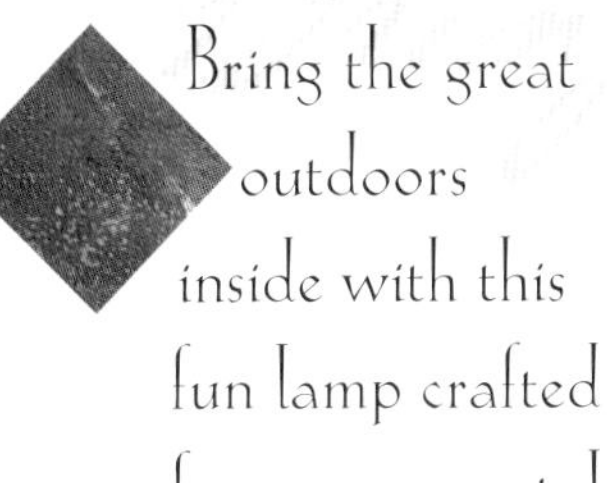

Bring the great outdoors inside with this fun lamp crafted from scrap metal.

Designer, *Jean Tomaso Moore*

MATERIALS

- Templates (see page 135)
- Piece of rusty sheet metal, 12 x 33 inches (30.5 cm x 83.8 cm)
- Piece of 2 x 4 lumber
- Water-based, mat-finish, spray acrylic sealer
- 4 wooden balls, 1½ inches (3.8 cm) in diameter
- 4 wood screws, ¾ inch (1.9 cm) long
- ½-inch (1.3 cm) copper pipe, 18½ inches (47 cm) long
- Lamp kit, including nuts and washers
- Lamp anchor weight, 3-inch (7.6 cm) diameter
- Acrylic craft paint in black, ruby-red metallic, and bronze or gold metallic
- Plain lamp shade
- Piece of aluminum flashing, 3 x 5 inches (7.6 x 12.7 cm)
- Leaf-pattern rubber stamp
- Stamp ink

TOOLS AND SUPPLIES

- Pencil or fine-tip permanent marker
- Paper
- Cardboard
- Scissors
- Pencil or felt tip pen
- Masking tape
- Long-nose tin snips
- Short-nose tin snips
- Electric drill with small bit and ½-inch (1.3 cm) bit
- Grinding bit and/or electric engraving tool with small sanding bits
- Hammer
- Screwdriver or large nail
- Paintbrush
- Pipe cutter
- Plastic cup

INSTRUCTIONS

1. Transfer the template design to the paper, enlarging it as desired. Draw the tree first, then the base, then the moose, using the marker. Transfer it to the cardboard and cut it out with the scissors, being careful around the leg areas. Bend up the cutout on each side of the base to see how the design works.

2. Tape the cardboard cutout to the piece of rusty sheet metal, and draw around it with the pencil or marker.

3. Use the long-nose tin snips to cut out the design, and cut around the legs with the short-nose snips. Use the electric grinding or sanding bit to smooth the cut edges.

4. To make the lamp base stand up by itself, brace the piece of 2 x 4 lumber against the bend lines. Hammer the metal against the wood at the bend lines. The moose and tree should now stand up, supported by the base.

5. Spray a coat of the sealer over the entire surface of the metal base and let it dry.

6. Using the ½-inch (1.3 cm) bit, drill a hole through the base center for the threaded lamp pipe from the lamp kit.

7. Use the paintbrush to paint the four wooden balls with the bronze paint. Let dry.

8. Using the small bit, drill pilot holes into the four corners of the base. Attach the painted wooden balls to the underside of each corner, using the four wood screws. The balls will serve as feet and elevate the lamp to accommodate the base weight and wiring.

9. Attach the base weight between the feet. Thread the lamp pipe through the weight, and secure it with the washers and nuts from the kit.

10. Using the pipe cutter, cut the ½-inch (1.3 cm) copper pipe to size to serve as a decorative sleeve over the threaded lamp pipe.

11. Wire the lamp with wiring from the kit.

12. Mix the black, red, and bronze or gold paint in the plastic cup, creating a muddy color to complement the rusty tones of the lamp metal. Use the brush to paint a thin layer of the acrylic mix onto the rubber leaf stamp. Impress the design on the shade in an overall pattern. When it's dry, spray the shade with a light coat of sealer.

13. Print the leaf stamp on the 3 x 5-inch (7.6 x 12.7 cm) piece of aluminum flashing. Let it dry, then cut around it with the tin snips, leaving a small circular area at the base of the leaf.

14. With the screwdriver or large nail, punch a hole big enough to slip over the finial screw of the lamp into the leaf base. Paint the back of the leaf. When it's dry, spray a thin coat of sealer over the entire piece and let it dry. Slip the leaf over the finial screw, holding it in place by screwing on the finial cap that comes with the lamp kit. Bend up the leaf to cover the front of the cap.

Punched Tin Lamp Shade

A starry, starry night shines in this charming little shade. You can buy the decorative metal punches you'll need at your local craft store.

Materials

- 36-gauge aluminum sheet, 12 x 12 inches (30.5 x 30.5 cm)
- Template (see page 135)
- Black acrylic paint
- Clear acrylic, matte finish spray sealer
- Small table lamp with large, frosted globe-style bulb

Tools and Supplies

- Pencil
- Shears or heavy-duty scissors
- Scissors with decorative cutting edge
- 4 star-shaped punches in different sizes
- Pad of newspapers, ½-inch (1.3 cm) thick
- 2 small paintbrushes
- Stylus or dried-up ink pen
- Steel wool
- Tacky glue
- 2 clamp-style clothespins or paper clips

Instructions

1. Enlarge the shade pattern as needed. Lay the aluminum flat and trace the pattern onto it with the pencil. Cut out the shape with the shears, cutting outside the lines. Use the scissors with a decorative cutting edge to retrim the bottom of the shade so it will have a decorative cut. Make sure the shade fits over the lamp globe, covering it completely.

2. Put the metal on the newspaper. Use the largest star punch to randomly punch out four or five stars, and repeat the process with the other punches. As the size of the punch decreases, increase the number of stars you punch with it.

3. After you have as many stars as you want, make random dots on the shade with the stylus or pen.

4. Use a paintbrush to apply a coat of the black acrylic paint to the shade and let it dry. Use the steel wool to buff off most of the paint, leaving an antiqued effect.

5. Roll the aluminum into a cone shape. Apply the tacky glue to the ends of the shade and overlap them, using the clothespins or paper clips to hold the ends together until the glue has dried completely.

6. Spray with the clear acrylic matte-finish sealer. Let dry, then lower the shade over the globe of the lamp.

Designer, *Delores Ruzicka*

Light Switch Plate Trio

Mexican designs inspired these easy light switch plates, but don't be afraid to adapt other imagery you like, such as a favorite quilt pattern.

MATERIALS

- 30-gauge tin or other metal sheet, 8 x 12 inches (20.3 x 30.5 cm) (for one switch plate)

TOOLS AND SUPPLIES

- Templates (see page 136)
- Scissors
- Glue stick, water-soluble
- Tin snips
- Denatured alcohol
- Rag
- Small jewelry or hobby file
- Sandpaper, 0000 grade
- Steel wool
- Dressmaker's carbon paper
- Scribing tool
- Piece of plywood or fiberboard, 12 x 12 inches (30.5 x 30.5 cm)
- Piece of rubber, 12 x 12 inches (30.5 x 30.5 cm), or newspaper
- Assortment of punches, round and chisel-tipped
- Hammer

INSTRUCTIONS

1. Enlarge the template of your choice on a photocopier as desired. Cut the pattern out with the scissors, and glue it to the metal with dots of the glue stick.

2. Cut out the pattern with the tin snips. Remove the paper pattern and clean away any glue with the denatured alcohol and rag.

3. Remove sharpness from the cut edges with the file, and smooth the edges lightly with the sandpaper and steel wool, being careful not to scratch the surface.

4. Put the dressmaker's carbon paper on top of the metal, carbon side down, and put the paper pattern on top. Use the scribing tool to transfer the pattern of dots and lines to the metal.

5. Cover the plywood with the rubber or newspaper, and put the metal on it. Position the tip of the punch where the design indicates, and gently tap it with the hammer, raising a pattern in the metal but not piercing it. Work from both sides of the metal to create a raised or embossed effect.

6. Remove any remaining carbon with the rag and denatured alcohol.

Designer, *Ellen Dooley*

Tie Plate Candle Shades

The elegant forms of these candle shades recall luminarias, but with a decidedly modern twist. In this project, you'll combine a few ready-made items from the hardware store with stunning results.

Materials

- 4 tie plates*, all the same size, from the lumber section of the hardware store
- 12 to 20 lock washers, 7 mm size
- Empty jar lid

  *From the fastener section of the hardware store. Please note that quantities are for creating one shade.

Tools and Supplies

- Masking tape
- 2 pairs of sturdy pliers

Instructions

1. Remove all labels from the tie plates.

2. Align the holes of the tie plates. The position of the holes may vary slightly, so be sure to use a small piece of the masking tape to mark the top of each plate. This saves time later when you join the holes. Set the tie plates aside.

3. Treat the lock washers in much the same way that you treat a jewelry jump ring. Using a pair of pliers, grasp the lock washer to one side of the split. Then, using the second pair of pliers, gently open the lock washer. Do this by bending the washer laterally, rather than making it wider. Your work will go faster if you open one lock washer, and try it for size before you open all the washers you'll need.

4. Lay one tie plate on top of another, matching the taped ends. Slide the opened lock washer into a matching pair of holes in the tie plate. You'll probably need to play with the washers before you successfully join the two plates. To make it easier to slide the washer through the holes, you may need to increase the width that you've opened the lock washer.

5. Determine how many lock washers you'll need to fasten the four sides of your shade. You'll develop a rhythm as you open the washers needed to complete the shade.

6. Complete one side of the shade at a time, matching the taped ends as you go along. You are simply linking the tie plates to one another.

7. To finish the shade, close each lock washer by grasping each side of the split with the pliers, and gently returning them to a closed position.

8. Set a votive or pillar candle in the used jar lid inside the shade.

Designer, *Terry Taylor*

Petit Four Votive Candleholders and Candle Ring

These are great projects for learning how to use pop rivets, and a visit to a kitchenware store will net you all the ready-made molds you need. The votive candleholders look fabulous massed together. If you choose, you can craft the candle ring to hold nine candles for a unique menorah.

Designer, *Terry Taylor*

MATERIALS

- Assorted petit four molds, shallow and deep
- Quiche/tart pan with removable bottom
- Aluminum or steel pop rivets, ⅛ inch (3 mm)

TOOLS AND SUPPLIES

- Fine-tip permanent marker
- Hole punch for metal or awl
- Pop-rivet gun

INSTRUCTIONS

1. Make a hole in the center of a shallow mold with the punch or awl. If you're using an awl, test the size of the hole with a pop rivet. The rivet should fit snugly.

2. Set the shallow mold on top of the deeper one. Mark the center of the deeper mold and make a hole in it.

3. Use the pop-rivet gun to rivet the two molds together. To create more votive candleholders, repeat using as many molds as you want.

4. To make the candle ring, mark the positions of the desired number of holders on the ring bottom of the quiche pan.

5. Make holes in the ring with the hole punch or awl. Test the size of the hole with a pop rivet, which should fit snugly.

6. Mark the center of each shallow mold, and use the punch or awl to make holes in all of them.

7. Use the pop-rivet gun to rivet the molds to the ring.

Designer, *Terry Taylor*

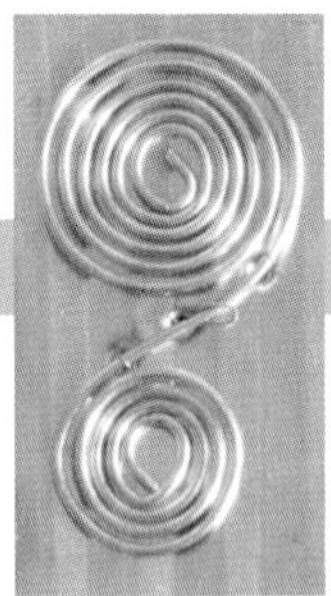

Boxes and Vessels

Dragon Box

Abracadabra! You don't have to be a wizard to make this fabulous box. The secret ingredients are aluminum oven liners from the grocery store.

Designer, *Cathy Smith*

MATERIALS

- Cigar box
- Paper
- Templates (see page 137)
- 2 large disposable oven liners, 15 x 18 inches (38 x 45.7 cm) each
- Large sheet of mat board
- Fabric
- Silver-colored piano hinge, ½-inch (1.3 cm), or two small hinges
- Silver-colored hasp
- #6 or #8 ¼-inch (6 mm) screws
- Oil base stain, dark brown
- Glass "jewels"

TOOLS AND SUPPLIES

- Fine-tip permanent marker
- Paper
- Awl
- Scissors
- Masking tape
- Mat board surface for cutting and embossing
- Blunt stylus with ¹⁄₁₆-inch (1.6 mm) tip, dried up ball-point pen, or chopsticks
- Blunt stylus with rounded, ¼-inch (6 mm) tip
- White craft glue
- Ruler
- Craft knife
- Heavy books or other weights
- Hacksaw
- Small screwdriver
- Extra-fine sandpaper
- Paintbrush, ½ inch (1.3 cm), soft
- Paper towels
- Jewelry glue

INSTRUCTIONS

1. With the marker, outline the top, sides, back, and front of the cigar box on the paper, along with their designs.

2. Remove the lid from the cigar box, and center the box on one of the oven liners. Avoid any lettering on the liner, but grooves in the material can be embossed out later. With the awl, score an outline of the bottom, then tip it over onto its front, and outline that. Repeat with the sides and back. Remove the box, and mark 1-inch (2.5 cm) and ½-inch (1.3 cm) extensions on the edges of the outline as shown in figure 1. Cut around the outline with the scissors.

3. Lay the lid on the second liner and score around the edges. Remove it and measure a 1-inch (2.5 cm) border all around. Score and cut out around the border with the scissors as shown in figure 2.

4. Photocopy the design templates, enlarging to fit the cutouts as necessary. Cut out the templates with the scissors. Put the box and lid cutouts on the mat board. Tape the templates in position. Outline them with the ¹⁄₁₆-inch (1.6 mm) point stylus, tracing directly through the paper with enough pressure to create a visible outline on the metal.

5. Remove the paper and deepen the outlines with the stylus with the ¹⁄₁₆-inch tip. This side of the metal is the front, the side that will show when you cover the box. Use the ¼-inch (6 mm) stylus to depress the background around the engraved pattern, working close to the outline without crossing it. Make ½-inch (1.3 cm), continuous strokes in the same

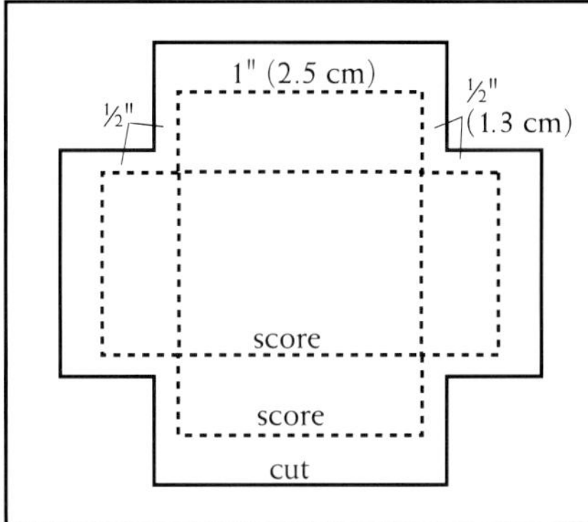

Figure 1

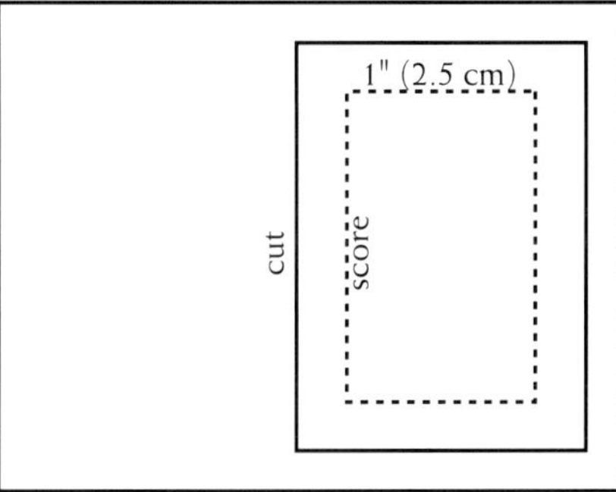

Figure 2

direction, as if you're coloring hard with a crayon. Emboss the background again, reversing the strokes' direction. To make the dragon wings or side patterns more prominent, turn over and emboss from the back inside the patterns.

6. To prevent the patterns from crushing, turn the embossed pieces face down and carefully fill cavities with the white craft glue. Don't let it overflow. Let dry overnight.

7. To cover the lid, lay the embossed piece face down, and trim the corners diagonally to the corners of the original scored outline. Coat the lid top with glue, and lay it glue-side down in the center of the notched aluminum. Put a squiggle of glue inside the four flaps that were created when you notched the corners, then fold them over at the score lines and smooth, removing any excess glue. Lay the covered lid face down on carpeting and weight with a book. Let dry.

8. Lay the embossed metal box cover face down and notch the corners as shown in figure 3. Coat the box bottom with glue, and center it on the metal. At the right and left edges of the front and back panels, fold the edges of the side flaps in on themselves, as indicated in figure 3.

9. Run a squiggle of glue inside the front, back, and side panels. Fold up the sides, wrapping the side flaps around the box corners. Fold up the front and back panels, and gently smooth over the box. Run a squiggle of glue on the flaps going over the top of the box. Fold them over. Wipe away excess glue and let dry.

10. Measure the inside bottom of the box, and cut the mat board to fit with the craft knife. Lay the board in the bottom. Measure the right and left sides of the box, and cut the board to fit, using the height of the front and back panels without including the "nub" that was left when you removed the lid. Put the side boards in place, measure the inside front and back panels, and cut the board to fit. Measure the underside of the lid. Subtract ⅜ inch (9.5 mm) from the front-to-back measurement and cut the board to size. This allows the lid to close without the liner showing.

11. Lay the fabric face down, and place the board on top. Trim the fabric around it with a ¾-inch (1.9 cm) margin, and notch the corners with the craft knife.

12. Remove the board, and cover one side with a uniformly thin coat of glue. Lay it glue side down on top of the face-down fabric. Put a thin bead of glue along the sides, and fold the fabric over, smoothing it over the board and wiping away excess glue. Repeat for the remaining boards and let dry.

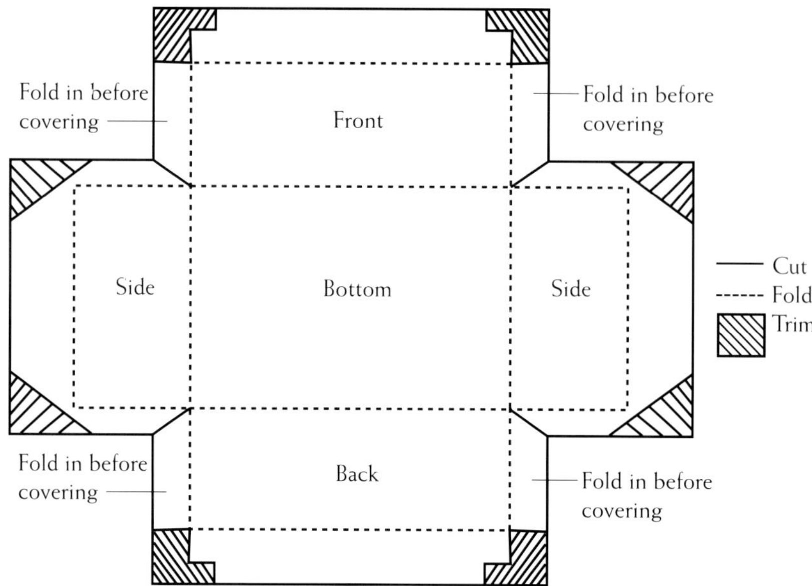

Figure 3

13. Apply glue heavily on the back of the covered boards, especially around the edges. Position the boards in the box in the same order you measured them. Remove excess glue, and smooth down until they stay in place. Glue the covered board in the center of the lid underside. Flatten it under a weight until it dries.

14. With the hacksaw, cut the piano hinge to the length of the box minus 1 inch (2.5 cm). Slip the top flap of the hinge between the underside of the box lid and the lid liner. Apply a little glue to the threads of the ¼-inch (6 mm) screws. With the screwdriver, screw in the hinge with them, working from the lid's lined side. Screw the other hinge flap to the back of the box. Apply glue to the hasp, and position it on the front of the box, then screw it in place.

15. Randomly dimple the background areas of the box pattern with the ¼-inch (6 mm) stylus. Gently sand it to achieve a brushed appearance. One side at a time, use the paintbrush to paint the box with the stain. Then immediately wipe most of it off with the paper towel, highlighting the patterns and giving the aluminum a warm silver tone. Allow to dry completely, then attach the glass "jewels" with the jewelry glue.

Trapezoid Photo Box

The unusual shape and delightful use of family photographs make this box a one-of-a-kind treasure.

Designer, *Polly Harrison*

MATERIALS

- 1 aluminum printing plate*
- Matte or gloss enamel paints, metallic sprays, and patinas of your choice, including matte black, brown, and green, and metallic gold and copper
- 1 piece of fiberboard, plywood, or plastic, 4 x 6 inches (10.2 x 15.2 cm)
- Polystyrene foam sheet, 2 x 3 feet (60 x 90 cm)
- 5 pieces of 1/16-inch (1.6 mm) thick clear plastic: (1) piece 5½ x 4 inches (14 x 10.2 cm); (3) pieces 5½ x 3 inches (14 x 7.6 cm); and (1) piece 3 x 4 inches (7.6 x 10.2 cm)
- 5 pieces of mat board, cut slightly smaller than the clear plastic pieces
- Color copies or scanned images of 5 photographs
- ⅛-inch (3 mm) pop rivets in ⅛, ¼, and ½-inch (3 mm, 6 mm, 1.3 cm) lengths
- Washers
- 2 x 4 lumber, 4-foot (1.2 m) length

*available at offset printing shops

TOOLS AND SUPPLIES

- Newspaper or a piece of cardboard
- Mineral spirits
- Paper towels
- Sharp scissors
- Handsaw
- Metal straight ruler
- Small paintbrush
- Fine-tip permanent marker
- Scoring tool (awl, metal punch, or large nail)
- Plywood work surface, 2 x 3 feet (60 x 90 cm)
- Metal T-square or triangle
- Needle-nose pliers
- Fine sandpaper
- Plastic cutting tool
- Craft knife
- Rubber cement
- Clothespins
- Power drill with ⅛-inch (3 mm) drill bit
- Pop-rivet gun
- Masking tape
- Protractor

INSTRUCTIONS

1. Lay the plate flat on the newspaper or piece of cardboard. Clean off any residual ink or images with the mineral spirits and paper towels, and smooth rough edges using the scissor handle.

2. Paint the matte or rough side of the aluminum plate. Use colors in a similar spectrum with light and dark contrasts. For an antique look, lightly spray or spatter the matte black, brown, or green paint over a wet base color. Let dry for a day.

3. Use the scissors to cut the plate into four pieces: 5 x 7 inches (12.7 x 17.8 cm) for the base; 4 x 6 inches (10.2 x 15.2 cm) for the bottom; 9 x 19 inches (23 x 48.3 cm) for the sides; and 8 x 10 inches (20.3 x 25.4 cm) for the lid.

4. Trim the piece of fiberboard, plywood, or plastic, with the handsaw to create a trapezoid. Take 1 inch (2.5 cm) off each side of the piece, making a shape that measures 4 x 6 x 4 x 4 inches (10.2 x 15.2 x 10.2 x 10.2 cm).

5. Use the marker to draw around the fiberboard in the center of the 4 x 6-inch (10.2 x 15.2 cm) piece of metal, and trim the metal. This piece will form the inside bottom of the box. Center the fiberboard on the 5 x 7-inch (12.7 x 17.8 cm) piece of metal, trace around it, and then score the lines with the scoring tool. Then cut out the corners, and cover the base with the metal. Set these two pieces of the box's bottom aside.

6. Lay the 9 x 19-inch (23 x 48.3 cm) piece of metal on the polystyrene foam, unpainted side up. Draw horizontal lines with the marker 1 inch (2.5 cm) from the top edge, and 1 inch (2.5 cm) from the bottom. With the T-square or triangle, working right to left, draw four vertical lines: one 4 inches (10.2 cm) from the right edge of the metal; one 4 inches (10.2 cm) from the first; one 6 inches (15.2 cm) from the second; and one 4 inches (10.2 cm) from the third. You should have a tab 1 inch (2.5 cm) wide on the left side.

7. Carefully score the lines with the scoring tool. Make 1-inch (2.5 cm) cuts with the scissors toward the center at the top and bottom of the score lines. Cut the top and bottom squares off the tab. With the tab to the left, fold the top 1-inch (2.5 cm) sections down and smooth with the scissors handle, forming the top inside edge of the box. Turn the metal over to the painted side.

8. Cut the plastic to size by laying it on the plywood work surface. Mark the cut lines. Position the metal ruler on a cut line and score it several times with the plastic cutting tool. Align the scored line with the table edge and snap it off. Snap off any unwanted bits with the needle-nose pliers, and sand the edge.

9. Use the ruler and craft knife to trim the images to fit in the mat board centers, surrounded by a margin of board. Glue them to the boards with the rubber cement. Let dry completely, and put the clear plastic squares on top.

10. Clean the mat/photo/plastic "sandwiches" of prints and debris. Lay them on the box sides ¼ inch (6 mm) from the baseline, secured with the clothespins. Drill four holes ½ inch (1.3 cm) from the corners through all the layers. Pop rivet them to the metal with a washer inside the box to hold them securely. Attach the other three photo panels (see fig. 1). Save the fifth for later.

11. Turn the metal to its unpainted side. Use the metal ruler to bend the bottom 1-inch (2.5 cm) sections up to a 45°

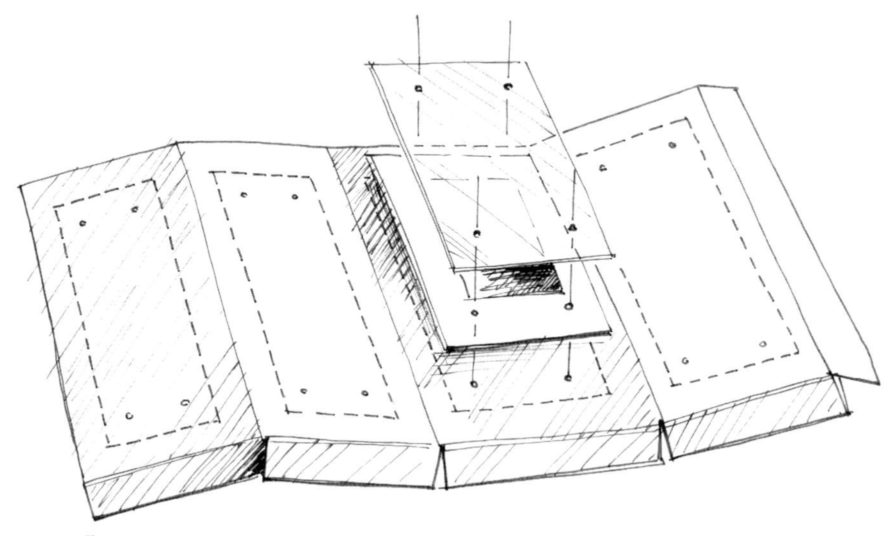
Figure 1

angle. Bend the vertical scored lines up at 45° angles to form the box walls. Insert the tab into the right edge under the top fold. Trim triangles out of the bottom tab from the corners of the 6-inch (15.2 cm) side, to adjust the overlap of the sharp angles of the bottom. Secure with a clothespin or tape. Hang the piece of 2 x 4 lumber off the edge of the work table, and slip the box over it. Drill holes and pop rivet the tab onto the side edge with a back washer. Allow three pop rivets for a box this size. Finish riveting the sides.

12. Fit the piece of metal cut for the inside bottom inside the box, painted side up. Trim until it fits snugly. Position the metal-covered base on the bottom and lightly tape it with masking tape to hold it temporarily in place. Slide the box onto the 2 x 4. Drill four holes in the corners of the base, and pop rivet with ½-inch (1.3 cm) rivets, using washers on the inside.

13. To make the lid (which should be slightly larger that the bottom), center the upside-down box on the back of the 8 x 10-inch (20.3 x 25.4 cm) piece of metal and draw around the edge. Straighten the shape with the ruler, and draw lines 1 inch (2.5 cm) out from the shape, then another set of lines ½ inch (1.3 cm) out from the previously traced shape (see fig. 2). Trim the metal at the outer lines and score the lines.

14. The lid for a trapezoid must have two 45° angle corners and two 135° angle corners. Align the edge of the metal ruler with the inside edge of each corner, check the angle with the protractor, and draw two lines out from each side at 45° angles. Check the angle of the other two corners.

15. Make tabs to put the lid together. Lay down the piece of metal, the long side at the bottom. Cut two horizontal lines on the left and right sides, on the score marks to the inside line. At the bottom, trim out the inside edge of the flap where the angle is too wide to make the flap straight. Fold the top and bottom flap sides down at the outside score lines, and smooth.

16. Center the fifth photo assemblage on the painted side of the lid and pop rivet it with the washers inside. Turn the lid over and use the ruler to fold the flaps and flap sides up. Fold the straight sides up, and fold over the flaps. Smooth with the scissors. Place the lid on the top of the box, and pinch the corners for a tight fit.

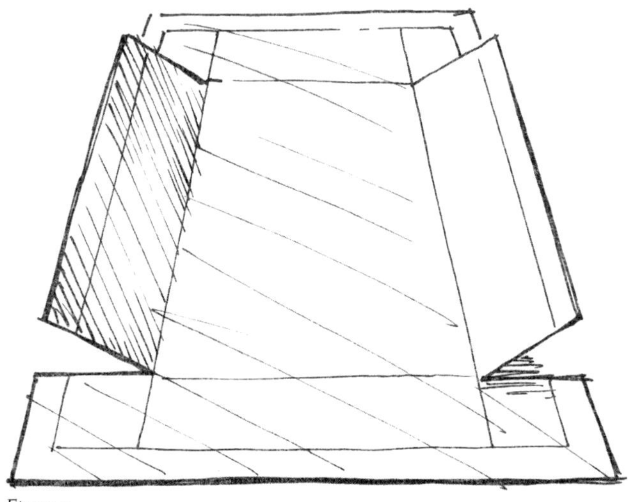
Figure 2

Hardware Cloth Baskets

Simply elegant as centerpieces and handy for storage, these stunning baskets are surprisingly easy to make.

MATERIALS

- Paper
- Hardware cloth with a ¼-inch (6 mm) mesh, 24 inches (61 cm) long
- Roll of 22-gauge steel wire

TOOLS AND SUPPLIES

- Pencil
- Ruler
- Scissors
- Wire cutters or metal shears
- Masking tape
- Scrap of 2 x 4 lumber, 6 to 8 inches (15.2 to 20.3 cm) long
- Wooden dowel, ¾ to 1-inch (1.9 to 2.5 cm) diameter, 12 inches (30.5 cm) long
- Bulldog clips or twist ties
- Needle-nose pliers
- Flat or half-round file

INSTRUCTIONS

1. Determine the size of the base you want for your basket. Eight inches (20.3 cm) square is a good size.

2. Use the pencil and ruler to measure an 8-inch (20.3 cm) square on the paper, and cut it out with the scissors.

3. Measure a 24-inch (61 cm) length of hardware cloth, and use the wire cutter or metal shears to cut it from the roll. Gently press the cut piece flat.

4. Center the paper pattern on the hardware cloth, and tape it down with the masking tape.

5. Now you'll cut away four corners from the hardware cloth square to create a cross shape. It's easy to make the cross accurate by cutting one section at a time with the wire cutters. Start the cut from the edge of the cloth and work to an outer corner of the paper square. Rotate the hardware cloth 90° and make an equivalent cut to the same corner. Repeat with the other three corners.

6. Remove the sharp, small stickers on all four edges of the hardware cloth with the wire cutters.

7. As it's termed in basket-making, you're now going to "upset" the sides of the basket. Using the scrap of 2 x 4 lumber as an edge, gently fold the sides up one at time.

8. To adjust the height of the sides, place the dowel along the top edge of a side and gently roll down the edge. Estimate how much cloth is needed to make the rolled edge, add it to the desired height of the sides, and cut off any excess. Don't roll the edge yet.

9. Use the wire cutters to cut a length of the steel wire about twice as long as the height of the basket sides.

10. Now you'll wire together the sides, two at a time, holding them together with the twist ties or bulldog clips while you work. Starting at the bottom of the basket, join the two sides with a short (½ inch [1.3 cm] or less) length of wire twisted onto the longer length of wire you cut earlier. Use the needle-nose pliers to twist the wire tightly, but not too tightly, or you'll break the hardware cloth.

11. Use the wire like you'd use thread, making an even whipstich up the side. Stitch every square or every other square, and tighten the stitch with the pliers as you go along. Don't make kinks in the stitching wire. Whipstitch up to the desired height, and leave the end of the wire free.

12. Whipstitch the remaining sides, leaving the wire ends free.

13. Now, roll the top of the side outward around the dowel. Press gently, and it will keep its shape. Use a twist tie to secure each end to the side of the basket at this point.

14. Use the free end of the wire (with which you stitched the sides) to whipstitch the rolled edge. Simply wrap the wire around a couple of times, and snip it off with the cutters.

15. Finish all edges in this manner.

16. Run your finger along the corners of the basket and at the ends of the rolled edges. Use the flat file to gently file off any burrs.

Designer, *Terry Taylor*

Woven Copper Basket

This handy little basket achieves uncommon glamour through a combination of unconventional materials and traditional weaving techniques.

Designer, *Joanne Wood Peters*

Materials

- 8-gauge, solid strand copper ground wire*, 20 feet (6 m)
- 18-gauge, braided copper ground wire*, 60 feet (18 m)
- Package of copper reinforcing strip, ¼-inch (6 mm) wide**
- Package of copper reinforcing strip, 5/32-inch (4 mm) wide**
- 30 copper-colored beads
- Twist tie

  *available at hardware stores

  **available at stained glass suppliers

Tools and Supplies

- Wire cutters
- Pliers
- Fine-tip permanent marker

Instructions

1. Use the wire cutters to cut the 8-gauge wire into 10 equal 2-foot (60 cm) lengths. Place the first length vertically to form the center spoke. Bend the next two spokes slightly at their centers and place one on each side. Continue to lay down pairs of spokes bent at a progressively smaller angle. Hold the first nine spokes together loosely with the twist tie, and lay the tenth and final spoke horizontally across them. Refer to figures 1 and 2 to check your work.

2. Use the wire cutters to cut a 40-inch (1 m) piece of the 18-gauge wire. Bend the piece a little off-center. Fold and loop it around the center spoke. Weave the top wire under the next spoke (fig. 3). Continue to weave, always passing the wire that's on top underneath the next spoke. After weaving the entire length of wire through the spokes, twist its ends together. Cut additional pieces of the 18-gauge wire of the same length, and use them to weave as needed, twisting the ends together. Weave until the woven part of the base measures 5 inches (12.7 cm) in diameter.

3. Create the sides of the basket by using two weavers in a continuous weaving technique called "chase weave." Using the pliers, bend the free ends of the spokes up at right angles. Taper the free end of the ¼-inch (6 mm) copper reinforcing strip with the scissors for about 6 inches (15.2 cm), narrowing it gradually toward the end. Taper 6 inches (15.2 cm) of the end of the ⁵⁄₃₂-inch (4 mm) strip, too.

4. Bend ½ inch (1.3 cm) of the ⁵⁄₃₂-inch (4 mm) copper strip around a spoke, and weave the strip halfway around the basket. Bend ½ inch (1.3 cm) of the ¼-inch (6 mm) copper strip around the spoke opposite to that of the first strip, and weave the ¼-inch (6 mm) strip around the basket. When you catch up to the ⁵⁄₃₂-inch (4 mm) strip, use it to continue weaving around the basket. You'll continue to "chase" one row of the ¼-inch (6 mm) strip with one row of the ⁵⁄₃₂-inch (4 mm) strip until there are five rows of each. Taper the ⁵⁄₃₂-inch (4 mm) strip above the point where you started, then weave it around a spoke and secure it.

5. Thread the 30 beads onto the free end of the remaining 18-gauge wire. Twist the end of the wire around the spoke where the ⁵⁄₃₂-inch (4 mm) strip ended, and weave the wire to the next spoke. Twist the wire once around the spoke, and push a bead into the space between the twist and the next spoke. Continue twisting the wire around spokes, placing a bead in every other space, until you reach the ¼-inch (6 mm) strip. Weave a row with the ¼-inch (6 mm) strip, then do another row with the wire and beads. Continue for three more rows, alternating the ¼-inch (6 mm) strip and braided wire. Cut off the wire and secure it to a spoke. Taper

the ⁵⁄₃₂-inch (4 mm) strip and bend it over the spoke. Weave three rows of ¼-inch (6 mm) strip and three rows of ⁵⁄₃₂-inch (4 mm) strip. Taper the ends and bend each around a spoke.

6. Measure 4½ inches (11.4 cm) up from the base of each spoke, marking the height with the marker. Use the pliers to bend the spokes outside the basket at a 45° angle. To finish the basket lip, bring one spoke behind a point two spokes to the right, and thread it out to the front, weaving its entire length around the basket. Trim the ends of the spokes to the same length.

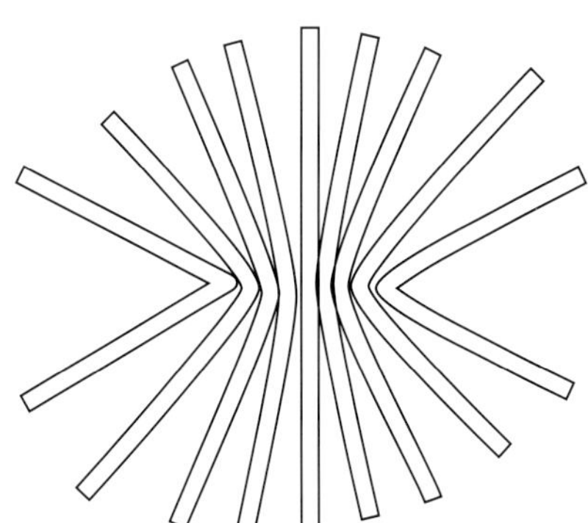

Figure 1

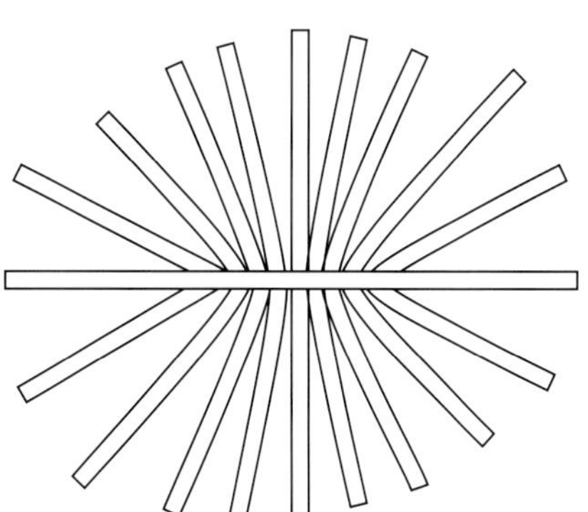

Figure 2

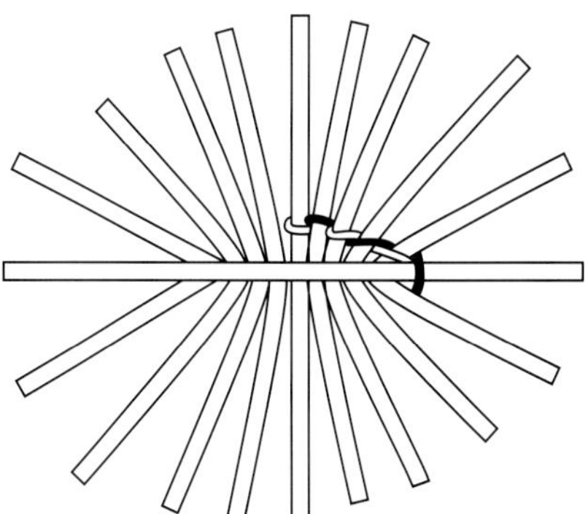

Figure 3

Woven Metal Bowl

This big, beautiful bowl is made from recycled aluminum printing plates, available for the asking from offset print shops. You can punch, crumple, score, rivet, and even cut this wonderful material with ordinary scissors. The key to using it is careful scoring and folding. You'll also have fun painting your own surface treatment in this project.

Materials

- 4 pieces of pre-painted aluminum printing plate: (1) 8 x 8 inches (20.3 x 20.3 cm); (1) 22 x 22 inches (56 x 56 cm); (1) 22 x 18 inches (26 x 71 cm); and (1) 22 x 6 inches (56 x 15.2 cm)
- Matte or gloss enamel paints, metallic sprays, and patinas of your choice, including matte black, brown, and green, and metallic gold and copper
- Piece of fiberboard, 6 x 6 inches (15.2 x 15.2 cm) square
- ⅛-inch (3 mm) pop rivets in ⅛, ¼, and ½-inch (3 mm, 6 mm, and ⅓ cm) lengths
- Tab from aluminum soft drink can
- Washers
- Polystyrene foam, 2 x 3 feet (60 x 90 cm)

Tools and Supplies

- Plywood work surface, 2 x 3 feet (60 x 90 cm)
- Newspaper or a piece of cardboard
- Mineral spirits
- Paper towels
- Sharp scissors
- Small paintbrush
- Power drill with ⅛-inch (3 mm) drill bit
- Pop-rivet gun
- Fine-tip permanent marker
- Straight metal ruler
- L-shaped metal ruler or T-square
- Scoring tool (awl, metal punch, or large nail)
- Clothespins
- Masking tape
- Yardstick

Instructions

1. Lay the plate flat on the newspaper or piece of cardboard. Clean off any residual ink or images with the mineral spirits and paper towels, and smooth rough edges using the scissor handle.

2. Paint the matte or rough side of the aluminum before cutting it to size, keeping it flat to avoid runs. Use colors in a similar spectrum with light and dark contrasts. For an antique look, lightly spray or spatter matte black, brown, or green paint over a wet base color. Paint the plate for the 22 x 18-inch (56 x 45.7 cm) piece in a contrasting color. Let dry for a day, then use the scissors to cut the pieces of plate as indicated above.

3. Make the base of the bowl by covering the fiberboard with the 8 x 8-inch (20.3 x 20.3 cm) sheet. Cut the corners and smooth any overlaps. Drill a hole through the center of one side, ½ inch (1.3 cm) from the edge. Working from the back, pop rivet through the base, the drink tab, and the washer to make a hanger.

4. On the back of the 22 x 22-inch (56 x 56 cm) piece, draw a cutting pattern with the ruler and marker, referring to figure 1 on page 76 for guidance. Measure 11 inches (28 cm) to the center of each side, and draw two lines to divide the metal into quarters. Center the base where the lines connect so it's like a diamond inside a square and the distance from corner to side is about 6¾ inches (17 cm). Trace the base square with the marker, and cut the four sides from the outside to the baseline with the scissors. Draw another square 2 inches (5 cm) outside the baseline. In the language of weaving, this is the "warp" line.

5. Working a quarter-section at a time, measure from the center of the warp line and draw a line from this point to the corner of the section. Measure six ¾-inch (1.9 cm) increments from the right of this center corner line, and repeat on the left side of the centerline to create the cutting pattern for the warp. Draw the other three quarter-sections. You now have a diamond in a square with

Designer, Polly Harrison

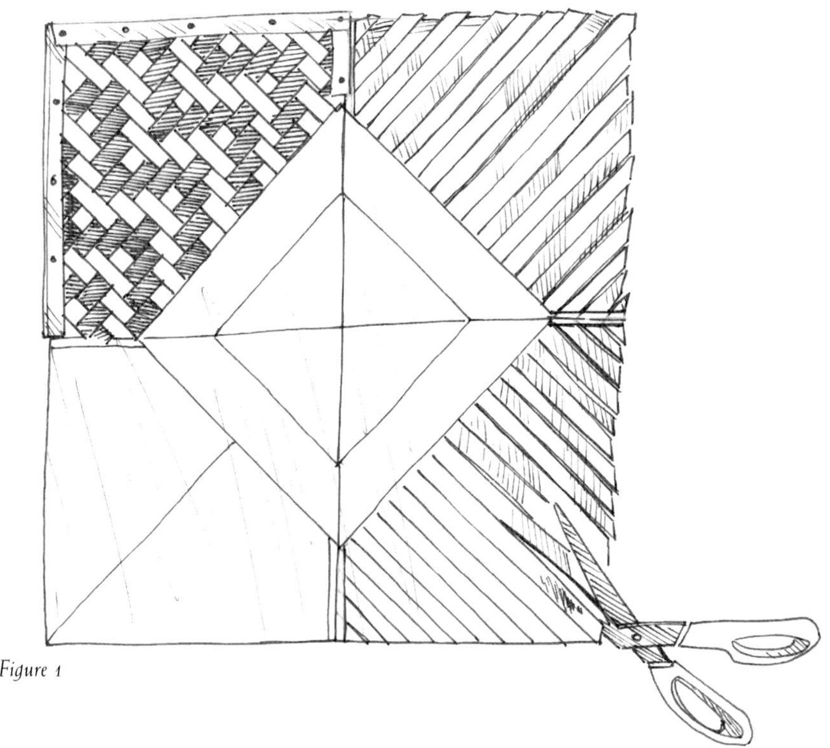
Figure 1

lines radiating out from the center (see fig. 1). On the original side cuts, draw a ¼-inch (6 mm) margin on each side of the cut to indicate where to stop cutting. Carefully cut the radiating lines to the warp line, trimming off any burrs. This is the warp on which you'll weave.

6. Cut 24 metal strips ¾ inch (1.9 cm) wide from the 22 x 18-inch (56 x 45.7 cm) plate. The nature of the metal makes a simple over-under tabby weave difficult, but it's easy to twill weave (over two, under two) and form a simple chevron pattern called the "water snake." Snake in a strip loosely and slide it up to tighten it. Weave from right to left, starting a strip under the right edge, weaving over two, under two, over two, etc. (see fig. 2) until you reach the left edge. You'll cut off the excess strip later.

7. Add another strip, beginning under, over two, under two, etc. Notice the pattern is moving to the right (see fig. 3). Add two more strips, beginning under. When you get to the fifth strip, weave it in the same way as the third strip, and the pattern will turn back the other way. The sixth strip matches the weave of the second strip. Trim all the strips even with the edges, saving the scraps to finish the corner. Continuing, the seventh strip matches the first, and the eighth strip begins the turn back. Finish the corner. Trim it and hold the weaving together with the masking tape. Finish weaving the other three sides.

8. Cut four strips 1½ inches (3.8 cm)

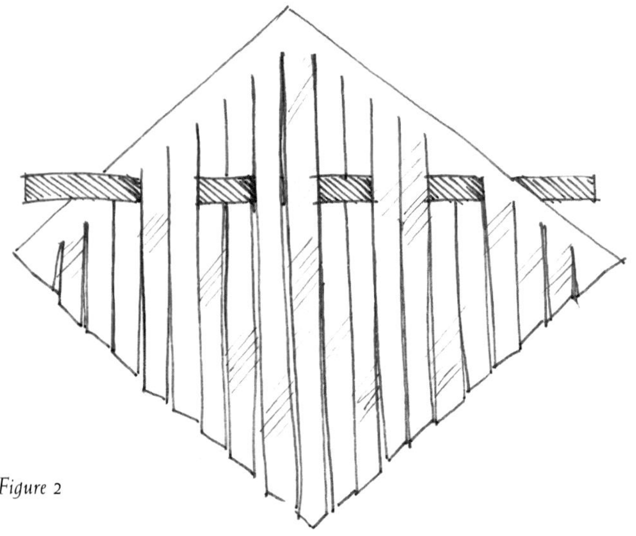
Figure 2

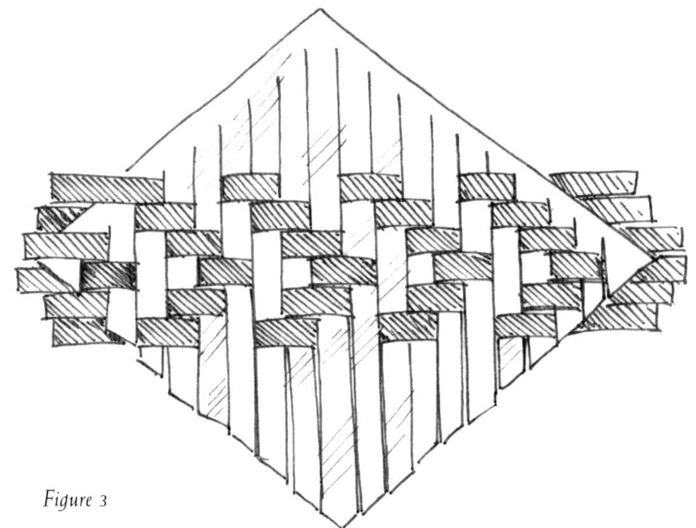
Figure 3

wide and 22 inches (56 cm) long from the 22 x 6-inch (56 x 15.2 cm) piece. Halve the strips to 1½ x 11 inches (3.8 x 28 cm). Lay the strips on top of the foam core, and use the metal ruler and scoring tool to score lines lengthwise through their centers. Bend the pieces up to a 45° angle and fold them to cover the ragged outside edges, smoothing with the scissor handles and holding them in place with the clothespins.

9. Make sure you have an even overlap on the corners. Drill holes on the corner overlap and pop rivet with a ¼-inch (6 mm) rivet, using a washer on the back. Tighten the edge if necessary and drill three holes, 3 inches apart, on each side of the corner and pop rivet in the same way using washers. Attach edging to the other three sides.

10. Turn the piece over to the back. The weaving pattern makes an uneven edge at the cut lines on the right side. Cover these edges with 2-inch (5 cm) weaving scraps, sliding them under the outside edge and holding them place with masking tape.

11. Decorate the inside of the bowl while it's flat with pop-riveted scraps of metal. For the center design, cut three 3½-inch (9 cm) squares and three 3-inch (7.6 cm) squares in contrasting colors. Center a small square on top of a large square in the center of the bowl bottom, with the points of the square aligned to the corners of the edges. Pop rivet the squares in each corner. Cut the four remaining squares from corner to corner to make triangles. Score ¼ inch (6 mm) down the smaller triangles' length and fold them over the larger triangles' long edges. Smooth with the scissors handle, and pop rivet the triangles to the four sections of the bottom, putting them point to point to extend the center square.

12. Integrate the base with the woven construction. Turn the bowl over to the back, center the base on the original line that you traced, and tape it to the base. Drill holes 1 inch (2.5 cm) from each corner of the base. Turn the piece over and pop rivet the base to the bowl, using ½-inch (1.3 cm) pop rivets with washers on the back.

13. Form the assemblage into a bowl shape by overlapping the sides, keeping the rough covered edge to the back. Attach clothespins to hold the shape. Use the yardstick to measure the sides corner to corner to make sure they're even. Tip the bowl on its side on the plywood work surface, and drill three holes in the overlaps (1½ inches [3.8 cm] from the center corner, 2½ inches [6.4 cm] from the center, and 3½ inches [9 cm] from the center). Pop rivet with washers to the back. Drill two holes where the metal overlaps on the edge, and pop rivet. Finish the other three sides.

14. If desired, use the brush and enamel paint to paint the pop rivets a color that blends with the basket.

Metal Strapping Basket With Crystals

Metal pallet strapping is used to tie heavy loads to pallets, and it's also the main ingredient in this beautiful container. You can buy strapping from industrial suppliers, but it's also plentiful and free for the taking in dumpsters, industrial parks, recycling centers, and scrap-metal yards. Choose pieces that aren't too rusty and brittle, and be careful of sharp edges.

Materials

- 11 to 12 feet (3.3 to 3.6 m) of ½-inch (1.3 cm) steel strapping
- ⅛-inch (3 mm) copper pop rivets, ¹⁄₁₆ to ⅛ (1.6 mm to 3 mm) inch grip range
- 3 clear plastic or crystal drops, 2-inch (5 cm), with matching ½-inch (1.3 cm) faceted beads
- 26-gauge copper or brass wire
- 3 copper- or brass-colored plastic beads, 6 to 8 mm

Tools and Supplies

- Wire brush
- Bull-nose metal snips (or a bench vise and a hacksaw)
- Ball-peen hammer
- Piece of chalk or fine tip permanent marker
- Hand-operated metal hand punch with ⅛-inch (3 mm) dies
- Pop-rivet gun
- Medium diagonal wire cutters
- Needle-nose pliers
- Vise grips
- Anvil or heavy piece of metal
- Masking tape
- Clear lacquer or acrylic spray

Instructions

1. The first step is to know and respect your material. Strapping is a tensile steel, meaning it's springy, hard, and sharp when cut. It also has great "memory," but will crack if folded in half. A little hand strength and the right cutting and punching tools are essential. Don't use improvised tools. Use a quality metal punch where indicated, and don't try to use a power drill. The material is too tough even for carbide bits, and it could seize up the drill.

2. Select straight lengths of strapping with a little rust patina. Scrape off excess rust flakes with the wire brush. Use the metal snips (or hacksaw and vise) to cut six lengths, each 20½ inches (52 cm) long. Snip off the corners and hammer out any burrs.

3. The six pieces will form the waistband, the three curved bands that make up the basket and scrolls with the crystal drops, and the two bands that function as the crisscrossed "feet" scrolls. Refer to figure 1 on page 80 as you work through the directions. The bands are numbered one through six, and the rivet holes are identified with the band number and a letter.

4. Use the chalk or marker to mark each strap with its assigned number and each hole with its letter. This will help you to keep the pieces and rivet holes straight. Hold each strap with the vise grips, and use the punch to make the holes.

5. Make strap no. 1 into a hoop by inserting a pop rivet from the outside at points 1A and 1G. Don't fasten it with the gun yet. Align hole 2A perpendicular to the join, and pop rivet everything together. Using the ball-peen hammer, flatten the inside of the rivet, as you'll do to every riveted connection. Use the diagonal wire cutters to cut out any half-popped rivets, and re-rivet.

6. Thread the long end of strap no. 2 back through the hoop and rivet hole 2C to hole 1D. Rivet from the outside in, and flatten the rivet. Rivet point 3A inside 1C. Thread through the long end, and rivet 1F to 3C from the outside in. Rivet 4A to 1E, and 4C to 1B. Cross straps 5 and 6 in the middle of the bas-

Designer, Aaron Kramer

ket bottom, and insert the rivet in the center hole and up all the B-holes of straps 2, 3, and 4. Make sure the rivet extends sufficiently so that after you've popped it with the gun, you can flatten it with the hammer.

7. Create the "feet" scrolls on straps 5 and 6. Grab ½ inch (1.3 cm) of a strap end with the needle-nose pliers, and roll it into a tight scroll toward the base of the basket, bending and making subtle adjustments. Do all four scrolls.

8. Bend down all four scrolls, making a nicely curved transition from the leg into the foot. Don't bend near the intersection at the bottom rivet or you may snap the connection. Level the legs.

9. Form the scrolls for the crystal drops the same way. Position the holes for the drops down at the scroll bottom, so the drops will hang nicely centered.

10. Finish the other end of the straps holding the drops, at the three points where they touch the basket's encircling waist strap. Use the vise grips or pliers to bend 1-inch (2.5 cm) flaps over the pop rivets on the waist strap, and tap them flat with the hammer.

11. Cover the crystals with masking tape, and spray the basket with a clear coat of lacquer or acrylic. Allow to dry and remove the tape.

12. Cut three 3-inch (7.6 cm) lengths of the 26-gauge wire. Thread a wire through a bead, and use the needle-nose pliers to fold an extra inch over and wind it in a small spiral at the base of the bead. Snip off the excess. Thread the wire through the hole in the scroll from the inside out, then thread it through the drop. Wrap the end of the wire around at the drop's top, or thread the wire back through the bead and wrap it, depending on the size of the hole in the bead. Snip off any excess and adjust the bead. Repeat for the other scrolls.

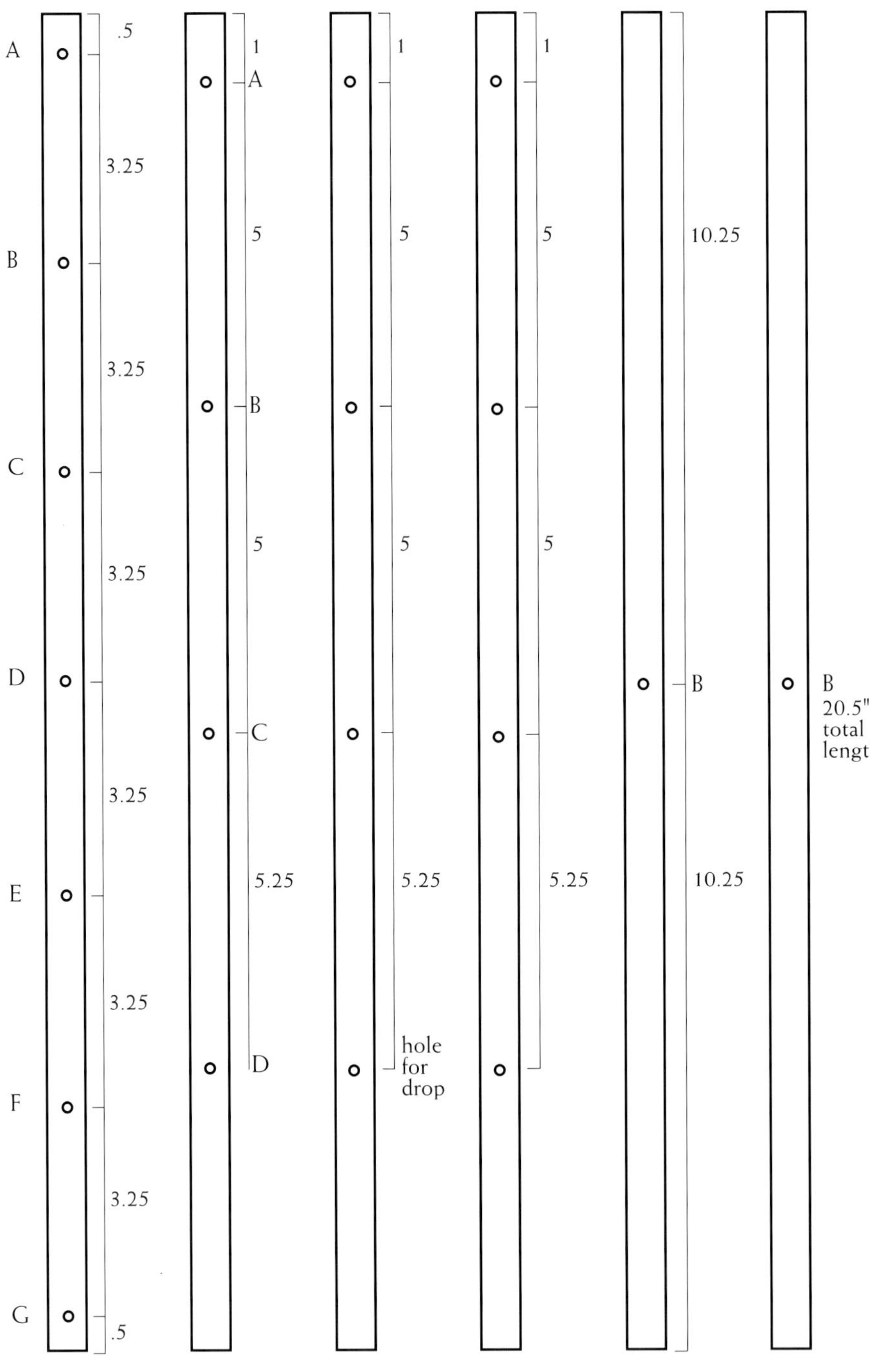

Textured Ivy Leaf Vase

Textured foil and a delicate mesh collar combine with leaves and copper binding in a vase that says, "Touch me!"

Designer, *Kathleen M. Anderson*

MATERIALS

- Pottery, glass, or plastic vase, 8 to 10 inches (20.3 to 25 cm) tall
- Lightweight copper mesh, 16 x 20 inches (40.6 x 50.8 cm), with ⅛ inch (3 mm) weave
- Quick-set molding compound, 3 lbs. (1.4 kg)*
- Kitchen-grade aluminum foil
- Burnt umber acrylic paint
- Metallic gold-toned finishing wax
- Soft, clean cloth
- Metallic antique copper acrylic paint
- Spool of 18-gauge bare copper wire
- 3 copper ivy leaves*
- Spool of 28-gauge bare copper wire

*available from craft store

TOOLS AND SUPPLIES

- Petroleum jelly
- Rolling pin or brayer
- Plastic bowl and water
- ½-inch (1.3 cm) paintbrush
- Paper towels
- Fabric glue
- Fine-tip permanent marker
- Ruler
- Drill and ¹⁄₁₆-inch (1.6 mm) drill bit
- Wire cutters
- Needle-nose pliers

INSTRUCTIONS

1. Apply a little petroleum jelly over the vase exterior, and stand it on its head.

2. On a flat surface, use the rolling pin or brayer to smooth out the folds in the copper mesh.

3. Center the mesh over the vase bottom and mold it over the form. Bend any excess at the neck out of the way.

4. Following package instructions, mix a small amount of the molding compound with water in the bowl. With the vase upside down, apply the molding compound over the mesh, working halfway to the neck. Work quickly, mixing more as needed.

5. After an hour, extract the vase from the mesh. Mix more compound, and apply it over the mesh close to the top. Leave nice, even folds of mesh sticking out above the vase. You can reshape the mesh, but gently. Dry overnight.

6. Fold down the top edges of the mesh ⅛ inch (3 mm).

7. Ball up four 6-inch (15.2 cm) pieces of kitchen foil. Open the balls, separating them carefully to retain the wrinkles.

8. Using the paintbrush, paint the foil pieces with the burnt umber paint, a bit at a time. Gently wipe off the paint with a paper towel before it dries, changing the towel frequently. Allow to dry.

9. Tear off small, irregular pieces of the painted foil, and apply them to the dried compound surface. Overlap the pieces as you go and glue them in place, especially the edges. Turn the excess foil at the top to the inside or trim it even with the vase top.

10. Rub the gold-toned finishing wax on the foil with a finger. Let it dry, and buff it gently with a clean cloth.

11. Paint the inside of the vase with the metallic copper paint and let it dry.

12. Choose the "front" of the vase. Divide the vase into four equal parts. Mark each quarter with the fine-tip marker, using the ruler to measure 5 inches (12.7 cm) up from the table, to indicate the wrapped wire placement.

13. Drill two holes at each mark, one above the other, about ¼ inch (6 mm) apart.

14. Using the wire cutters, cut a continuous piece of 18-gauge wire that measures 3½ times the vase circumference. Cut four 8-inch (20.3 cm) pieces of the 28-gauge wire. Cross one end of the 18-gauge wire over the front pair of holes, lapping the wire over the holes about 1½ inches (3.8 cm). Run an 8-inch (20.3 cm) piece of wire through the top front hole to the inside of the vase and out the front bottom hole, securing the end of the 18-gauge wire. Repeat with all the holes around the vase until you've gone around three times. Cut off any excess with the wire cutters, and secure by twisting the free end around itself.

15. Drill two more holes in the front of the vase above and below the three wraps of 18-gauge wire, far enough from the first holes so you don't break through. With 12 inches (30.5 cm) of the 18-gauge wire, attach the three ivy leaves by going through the top hole to the inside of the vase and out the bottom hole. Twist to secure and coil the ends with the needle-nose pliers.

16. Arrange the three copper leaf stems to the side of the center front. Drill two more holes, and secure the stems with a 6-inch (15.2 cm) piece of 28-gauge wire.

Gathering Love Basket

This delightful basket uses antique ceiling tin and recycled pallet strapping in a charming design that pays homage to the past. You can solder the base and legs on, or use twisted heavy-gauge wire instead.

Designer, *Kathryn Arnett*

MATERIALS

- Antique, recycled ceiling tin, approximately 40 x 40 inches (1.1 x 1.1 m)
- 4 short machine screws, nuts, and small washers, ¼-inch (6 mm) diameter
- Piece of metal pallet strapping, 28 inches (71 cm) long
- Roll of baling wire
- 4 brass or copper rods, ¼-inch (6 mm), each 36 inches (91.4 cm) long
- Heavy gauge wire, 3/16 or ¼-inch (4.8 or 6 mm) diameter, 12 feet (3.6 m) (optional)

TOOLS AND SUPPLIES

- Metal measuring tape
- Fine-tip permanent marker
- Tin snips or metal shears
- File
- Bull-nose pliers
- Hammer
- Rolling pin or other solid, cylindrical object
- 2 vise grips
- C-clamps
- Table vise (optional)
- Power drill with ¼ and ⅛-inch (6 and 3 mm) drill bits
- Screwdriver
- Needle-nose pliers
- Wire cutters
- Hacksaw
- Short section of PVC pipe, 4-inch (10.2 cm) diameter
- Liver of sulfur solution or other blackening agent* (optional)
- Sandpaper (optional)
- Scouring powder
- Denatured alcohol
- Rags
- Electric soldering iron, or soldering copper (optional)
- Hand-held propane torch (optional)
- Paste flux for lead-free soldering (optional)
- Flux brush (optional)
- Lead-free solder (optional)

*available from craft and metals suppliers

INSTRUCTIONS

1. Use the metal measuring tape and marker to mark 20½ inches (52 cm) on the lower edge of the tin (see fig. 1). To indicate the outer arc, measure 30 inches on the tape and "bow" it to form the arc. Holding the tape in place on the tin, lightly trace around the arc with the marker. Repeat the process to mark the inner arc; create a 6½ inch (16.5 cm) "bow" with the measuring tape, position it in the middle of the 20½ inch (52 cm) edge of the tin, and trace around it with the marker. Cut out the tin with the tin snips or metal shears and lightly file the edges.

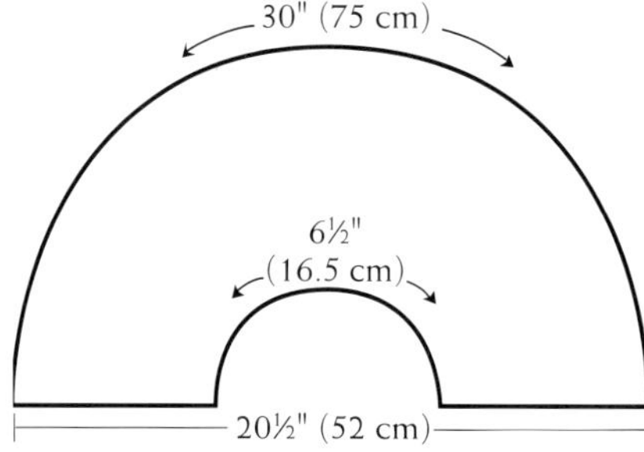

Figure 1

2. Cut out six 2 x 2-inch (5 x 5 cm) squares from the ceiling tin scrap. Draw a heart shape in each square. Cut them out with the shears, file the edges, and set aside.

3. Use the bull-nose pliers to bend a ¼-inch (6 mm) margin around the edge of the large tin piece, toward the unpainted side. Work around the large arc, the two straight edges, and then the small arc. Tap the bend lightly with the hammer, moving from section to section, keeping the bend even. Hammer it flat.

4. Round the tin around the rolling pin, lapping the straight edges ½-inch (1.3 cm) over each other to make a lampshade form. Secure the top and bottom of the join with the vise grips.

5. Place the lapped side flat on the table and secure the tin to the table with the C-clamps. Holding the unclamped side, use the power drill to create four ¼-inch (6 mm) holes, spaced evenly along the lapped edges, and fasten the tin together with the screws, nuts and washers, tightening with the screwdriver and pliers. The seamed side is the basket's "back."

6. Remove the vise grips. Put the "front" face down on the work surface and secure. Drill a ⅛-inch (3 mm) hole in the midpoint of the front, ½ inch (1.3 cm) from the edge, plus one hole 3 inches (7.6 cm) to the right and one 3 inches (7.6 cm) to the left. Turn the basket over and drill three similarly-spaced holes on the back side.

7. Drill five evenly spaced ⅛-inch (3 mm) holes, ½ inch (1.3 cm) from the edge of the small end of the basket.

8. Using the hammer and the edge of the table or vise, hammer the pallet strapping into a zig-zag with 2-inch (5 cm) bends. Make a curl on each end with the needle-nose pliers. Drill two ⅛-inch (3 mm) holes, one above the other, ½ inch (1.3 cm) apart, over the curl on each end of the zig-zag "handle."

9. To drill ⅛-inch (3 mm) holes in the sides of the basket for the handle, put the basket on its side. Drill one hole ½ inch (1.3 cm) from the edge, and a second hole ½ inch (1.3 cm) below the first hole. Drill a matching pair of holes on the other side.

10. Cut the baling wire with the wire cutters as follows: (6) 6-inch (15.2 cm) pieces, (5) 3-inch (7.6 cm) pieces, and (5) 8-inch (20.3 cm) pieces.

11. Shape five of the 3-inch (7.6 cm) pieces of wire into U-shapes. Insert the ends of a U through two side holes, then out through two holes at the end of the basket handle. Flatten the wire inside with the needle-nose pliers. Twist the ends together two or three turns on the outside with the bull-nose pliers, and make wire "curls" with the free ends of the wire using the needle-nose pliers. Repeat on the other side with another U and the other end of the handle. Set the other three U shapes aside.

12. Working with the five straight 8-inch (20.3 cm) wires, make a curl with the needle-nose pliers on one end of each wire. Insert the straight ends through the five drill holes around the bottom, with the curl on the outside and the loose ends dangling through the open basket bottom. Bring the free ends together. Cut a 6-inch (15.2 cm) piece of baling wire with the wire cutters and wrap it six times around the bunched ends. Curl the ends with the needle-nose pliers.

13. Use the hacksaw to cut four 36-inch (91.4 cm) lengths of rod. Round it over the PVC pipe to create an arc, and use the pliers to bend one end into a "foot." Repeat for the other two legs. If you wish, use the liver of sulfur or other blackening agent according to the manufacturer's instructions to darken the metal. Sand lightly to achieved an "aged" look.

14. Round the fourth piece of rod into a circle. File the ends and clean with the scouring powder and denatured alcohol using a rag. Flux and solder the ends of the rod together (for detailed directions on soldering, see page 23). Clean, flux, and solder the three legs to the circle to make a tripod. Cover the soldered join of the circle with one of the legs when you solder it on.

Note: If you don't want to solder, use the hacksaw or wire cutters to cut four pieces of the heavy-gauge wire, each 36 inches (91.4 cm) long. To make the base, wind a 36-inch (91.4 cm) piece of wire around to make a circle with a 15-inch (38 cm) circumference. Wrap the free end around itself with the pliers and secure.

To make the legs, take a piece of wire and bend 26 inches (66 cm) of it accordion-style, back on itself, then use the last 10 inches (25.4 cm) to wrap all the strands together. Repeat to make the other two legs. Cut three 8-inch (20.3 cm) pieces of baling wire with the wire cutters, and use them to wire the legs to the circle, cutting off any excess.

15. Set the basket in the base, aligning one leg with the seam. The tripod base roughly divides the basket into three sections. Hold the basket straight with one hand, and use the chalk to mark pairs of holes at the midpoints of the basket "sections", one hole above and one below the circular rod. Take the basket out of the base and drill ⅛-inch (3 mm) holes at the marks.

16. Put the basket back inside the base, and use the three remaining U-shaped, 3-inch (7.6 cm) pieces of wire to attach the basket to the base with the same process as step 11.

17. Drill a ⅛-inch (3mm) hole in each cut-out heart. Curl one end of a 6-inch (15.2 cm) piece of wire with the needle-nose pliers. Insert the straight end into a rim hole, through the front and into the basket. Bring the wire out over the top of the basket, and use the needle-nose pliers to wrap it around the dangling part of the wire over the heart. Repeat with the other hearts.

18. Wash the piece. After it dries, spray it with with clear, water-based acrylic matte spray to seal the metal.

Mud Tray Vessels

It's hard to believe that these gorgeous containers are made from something called a mud tray! Look in the building materials and fastenings departments of your hardware store for the off-the-shelf items you need to assemble this incredibly easy project.

Materials

- Mud tray
- 4 drawer pulls
- 4 screws* shorter than those included with the drawer pulls
- Small washers* matched to the screw size, ½-inch (1.3 cm) wide or less
- 5 fender washers including 1 large, 2 smaller, and 2 smallest
  *You'll need 8 screws and 8 washers if you select drawer pulls with two points of attachment apiece.

Tools and Supplies

- Fine-tip permanent marker
- Electric drill with drill bit sized to match the screws
- Screwdriver
- Industrial-strength metal glue or jewelry glue
- Piece of scrap wood the length of the mud tray
- C-clamps or other clamps
- Craft knife

Instructions

1. Turn the mud tray upside down. Position the drawer pulls at the corners, and use the marker to trace around the base of each pull.

2. Match the size of the drill bit to the size of the screws. Mark the center of the outlines you've made of the drawer pulls, and drill a hole at each center mark.

3. Attach the drawer pulls to the bottom, threading a washer on each screw and using the screwdriver to attach each pull.

4. Decorate the vessel by gluing on the fender washers in descending sizes. Clamp them in place with the piece of wood and C-clamps while they dry overnight.

5. Use the craft knife to clean off any messy bits of glue that squeezed out around the washers, being careful not to scratch the metal.

Designer, *Terry Taylor*

JESTER'S BOX

This spirited little box is an imaginative use of readymade objects off the shelves of any home improvement store, with a dash of whimsy added. Careful cutting and bending of the copper helps achieve a finished look.

Designers, *Doug Hays and Penny Cash*

MATERIALS

- Box and lid templates (see page 136)
- Sheet of copper roofing flashing, 8½ x 11 inches (21.6 x 28 cm)*
- Scrap leather or canvas, ¼-inch (6 mm) thick, 6 x 6 inches (15.2 x 15.2 cm) square
- 2 lengths of hardwood, 2 x 2 x 6 inches (5 x 5 x 15.2 cm) each
- 4 brass-plated robe hooks for legs
- 20 ⅛-inch (3 mm) pop rivets, ½-inch (1.3 cm) long
- Decorative brass hinge, 1½ inches (3.8 cm) long
- Lamp finial and screw
- 2 small brass corner protectors
- 8 brass cap nuts, #6

  *available from a roofing or gutter supplier

TOOLS AND SUPPLIES

- Scissors
- Scribe
- Tin snips, or preferably a set of 3 aviation shears for straight cuts, right curves, and left curves
- Shears
- Flat file or grinding wheel
- Power drill with ⅛-inch (3 mm) drill bit
- Mounted grinding stone for drill, 1-inch (2.5 cm) size
- Pop-rivet gun
- Small ball-peen hammer
- Half-round fine file
- Chisel
- Needle-nose pliers
- 2-part epoxy
- Fine-tip permanent marker

INSTRUCTIONS

1. Enlarge the templates on a photocopier, keeping them in proportion, so they both fit on one 8½ x 11-inch (21.6 x 28 cm) sheet of paper. Use the scissors to cut them out outside the solid outline. Don't cut the dotted lines; you'll scribe them later.

2. Use the scribe to outline the box and lid on the copper sheet, tracing the outline with enough pressure to leave marks on the metal.

3. Use the tin snips or shears to carefully cut out the box portion. Smooth the edges with the flat file and the grinding stone mounted on the drill. Gently hammer the edges flat.

4. Cut out the lid carefully and slowly. Clean up the edges, and shape the curves with the half-round fine file and grinding stone. Lightly hammer the edges flat.

5. Scribe the dotted lines from the box and lid templates to create the folding lines. Don't score the lid yet.

6. To prepare the box for folding, dull the chisel with the flat file so it won't cut through the copper. Practice chiseling lines on scrap copper backed with ¼-inch (6 mm) layers of leather or canvas, lightly tapping the chisel with the hammer so the lines just crease the metal. The lines will help make straight bends in the metal.

7. Once you've practiced, work on top of the leather or canvas, and use the hammer and chisel to tap indentations along the scribed lines of the box and lid. Be careful not to punch through the copper, and keep in mind that the side you're working on will be the inside of the pieces. Start with the flaps labeled A on the template, then tap the square that makes up the bottom. At this point, the box is starting to take shape.

8. With the pliers, bend the flaps in on the sides slightly past a 90° angle.

9. Sandwich the copper between the two pieces of wood. Resting the bottom on the edge of the work surface, bend it up along the chiseled line (see fig. 1). Make several small bends to produce an even, straight bend. Finish the bend by hand, and repeat the procedure on all sides.

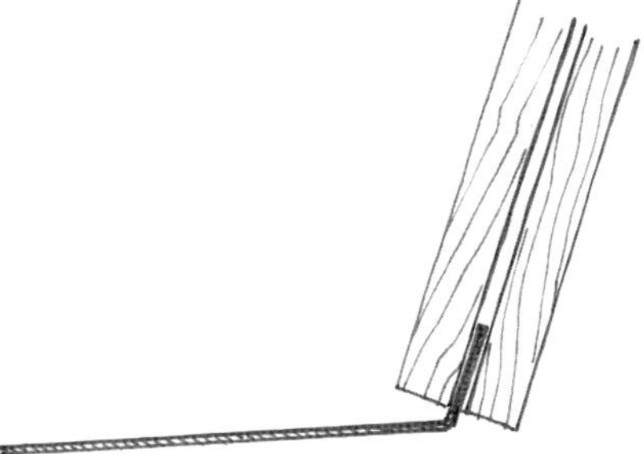

Figure 1

10. Fold the box so the rivet tabs are located inside the box, and form the box shape by hand.

11. Turn the box upside down and square up the bottom edge with several light hammer taps. Use one of the blocks for support.

12. Before squaring up the sides, rivet the box together. Using the electric drill and appropriate bit, drill a hole ¾ inch (1.9 cm) from the top of the back side and ³⁄₁₆ inch (4.8 mm) from the corner (see fig. 2). Drill the hole through the side and tab, and pop rivet the back plate to the side tab. Repeat on the other three corners.

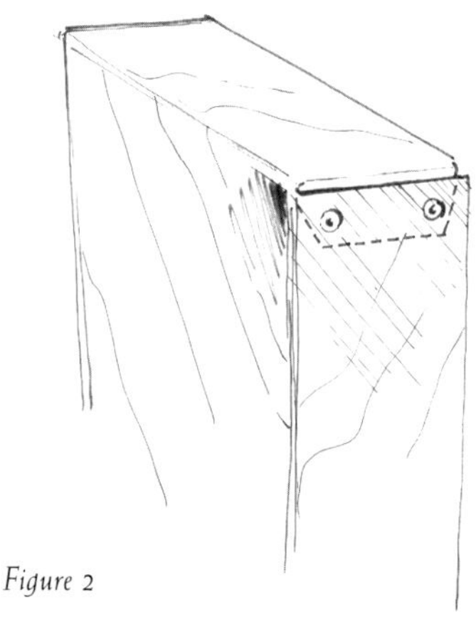

Figure 2

13. Using the hammer and a 2 x 2 x 6-inch (5 x 5 x 15.2 cm) piece of wood, form up the side joints (see fig. 3).

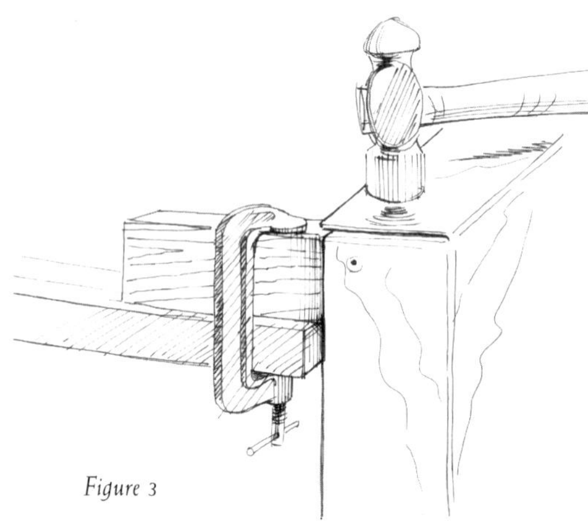

Figure 3

14. Set the box upright on a level surface. If it wobbles, level out the bottom with the hammer and wood pieces. Set the box upright and file or grind down any high spots on the rim.

15. Turn the box over and fit the robe hooks on the bottom, marking the rivet holes. Drill the holes for the rivets and pop rivet the legs on. Stand the box up. If it's wobbly, file or grind the bottom of the feet to level it.

16. Now you'll score and bend the lid. Turn the box upside down and use it as a guide to scribe the bending lines on the lid. Since the lid won't fit if it's a bit small, chisel the bending lines a little outside the scribed outline of the box.

17. After you've scored the lid, bend it as you bent the box. Fold the two small tabs on the front top of the sides labeled B on the template, folding them over the face of the lid. Epoxy them in place if desired.

18. Fit the lid on the box, positioning it to open and close easily.

19. Center the hinge on the back and mark the holes. Drill the holes in the lid and box, enlarging the holes in the hinge if necessary. Pop rivet the hinge onto the box.

20. Find the center point of the lid top and mark it. Drill a hole large enough to accept the finial screw, and mount the finial on top of the box.

21. Epoxy the corner protectors on the front corners of the lid. Allow to dry.

22. Turn the box on its back, and epoxy the #6 cap nuts over the pre-drilled holes in the corner protectors and on the ends of the scalloped lid decoration. Repeat on both sides.

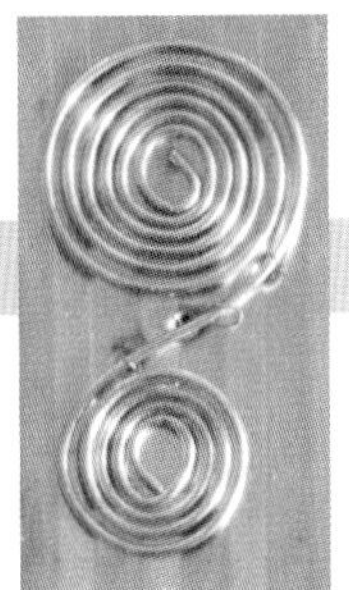

Good Fortune Earrings

These delightful earrings are simplicity itself to make with a few folds of metal and paper.

Designer, *Pei-Ling Becker*

Materials

- 2 pieces of copper foil, each 5 x 2 inches (12.7 x 5.1 cm)
- Piece of decorated paper, 6 x 2 inches (15.2 x 5.1 cm)
- Metallic thread, rust-colored, two 12-inch (30.5 cm) pieces
- Small beads, 12 blue and 12 gold
- 2 earring backs

Tools and Supplies

- Scissors
- Jewelry cement

Instructions

1. Fold each foil sheet into a fan shape with seven creases, with one end pinched closed and the other end fanned open.

2. Use the scissors to cut the decorated paper into two pieces measuring 3 inches (7.6 cm) in width and 2 inches (5.1 cm) in length. Cut each piece again into six pieces, each measuring ½ inch (1.3 cm) in width and 2 inches (5.1 cm) in length.

3. Fold the ½-inch (1.3 cm) pieces so that each piece measures ¼-inch (6 mm) wide by 2 inches (5.1 cm) long.

4. Slide a piece of folded paper into each crease of the folded metal, so that the folded edge of the paper is facing outward.

5. Wind a piece of the metallic thread around the "handle" of the fan to bind everything together. Tie a knot in the thread to secure it.

6. Bead by bead, slip a bead onto about ½-inch (1.3 cm) of the thread, knot it on the end, and cut the thread. Knot another piece of thread on the earring, slip on a bead, and repeat until you've attached six blue and six gold beads to the earring.

7. Repeat steps 5 and 6 with the second earring.

8. Glue the earring backs to the backs of the fans with the jewelry cement, and let dry.

Tin Can Cuff Bracelets

If the can fits, wear it! Inventive curling and great graphics transform the tin cans in your pantry into high-fashion cuffs. Load them on for maximum impact. You'll also create a useful safety tool as part of this project.

Designer, *Terry Taylor*

MATERIALS

- Tin cans with ribbed sides
- Spare piece of steel, such as a wrench handle or knife handle
- Metal adornments of choice

TOOLS AND SUPPLIES

- Safety can opener
- Wire cutters
- Tin snips or metal shears
- File
- Scouring pads
- Fine-tip permanent marker
- Bench vise
- Hacksaw or band saw
- Hammer
- Needle-nose pliers
- Hole punch for metal or awl (optional)
- Pop rivets and pop-rivet gun (optional)
- Solder, flux, and soldering iron (optional)
- Piece of PVC scrap or rolling pin (optional)
- Anvil (optional)

INSTRUCTIONS

1. Remove the top and bottom of the can with the can opener. To remove the wire rim, put the can on its side and use the can opener to remove it. Alternatively, use the wire cutters at the points you need to cut through the wire rim, and finish removing the rim by cutting it away from the body of the can with snips or shears. Never use your snips or shears directly on the wire rim, or you'll ruin them.

2. Smooth the cut metal edges with the file and scouring pads, making absolutely sure there are no burrs or jagged edges before you try the can on your wrist for size.

3. Once you know the can fits, decide how wide you want to make the bracelet. Different cans have different ridge patterns, and your can's specific pattern will help you determine the bracelet width. If you're thinking about buying something in a grocery store just to obtain the can, feel the paper label for the ridge pattern underneath.

4. Mark the width of the bracelet with the marker, and use the snips to remove the excess from the can.

5. Unless you'll be cutting and curling the edges of the bracelet, or using the entire filed-and-scoured can to create your bracelet, it's essential for you to create "safe edges" on the cut metal edges. To make your safety edge tool, secure a spare piece of steel, such as a worn-out wrench handle or stainless steel kitchen knife handle (with the blade removed), in the bench vise. Use the band saw or hacksaw to cut a ⅛-inch (3 mm) slit in the steel.

6. Insert the edge of the can into the safety edge tool you've made, and work your way around the can, bending over the edge at an angle less than 90°. Work around the edge a couple of times, increasing the angle of the bend each time. Avoid making the angle too sharp too quickly, or you may tear the edge of the can. Use the hammer to finish flattening the folded-over edge. You've now made a basic cuff bracelet.

7. If you're going to punch decorative holes, do it before curling the edges. Support the bracelet with the scrap of PVC pipe to keep it from collapsing while you hammer the punch against the can. If you use an awl or grommet punch instead of a conventional metal punch to create the holes, you'll need to use the file or scouring pad to eliminate the rough or burred edges around the holes.

8. To curl the edges as shown in the photo below, use the tin snips or shears to trim the can so that there is a ridged central portion bordered by unridged metal on both sides. Fringe the flat borders of the metal with the tin snips up to

the ridged section, making the cuts ⅛- to ¼-inch (3 to 6 mm) apart. Grasp one section of the fringe at a time with the needle-nose pliers, and roll and curl it as desired. Continue around the entire bracelet, varying the tightness of the curl.

9. Possibilities abound for decorating your bracelet. Use an awl to create tiny holes for "sewing" beads in place with beading wire. Cut out fun shapes from different metals with the tin snips, or use images from other tins. Tack solder or pop rivet premade metal forms to the bracelet. The designer even raided his clip-on Christmas tree candles for the attractive gold medallions attached to one bracelet (see photo below). The sky's the limit! Just be sure create safe edges where necessary, and to smooth burrs from any punched holes with your file or scouring pads.

Faux Pewter Bookends

The rich look of pewter is easy to achieve when you use a simple hammering technique to make these handsome bookends from aluminum flashing.

Designer, *Cathy Smith*

MATERIALS

- 2 large office-style metal bookends
- ¾-inch- (1.9 cm) thick hardwood board, at least 6 inches (15.2 cm) wide
- Mat board, enough for two 8 x 10-inch (20.3 x 25.4 cm) pieces
- Piece of aluminum flashing, 7 x 10 inches (17.8 x 25.4 cm)
- ½-inch (1.3 cm) nails with large heads
- Silver upholstery tacks

TOOLS

- Fine-tip permanent marker
- Ruler
- Handsaw
- Craft knife
- Awl or small flat-head screwdriver
- Aviation shears
- Industrial-strength adhesive
- Heavy books or other weights
- Small ball-peen hammer
- Cloth measuring tape
- Needle-nose pliers
- Fine sandpaper

INSTRUCTIONS

1. Measure the upright faces of the bookends. Mark the board and saw off two wood pieces ½ inch (1.3 cm) wider and 2 inches (5 cm) taller. Saw the two top corners off both pieces, creating two bottom-heavy hexagrams. With the marker, trace the wood pieces on the mat board and cut them out with the craft knife.

2. Lay one wood piece on the flashing. With the awl or screwdriver, score around the wood into the aluminum, allowing a 2-inch (5 cm) overhang on the sides. Don't score so deeply that the aluminum breaks when bent.

3. Carefully measure the thickness of the edge of the wood piece; ¾-inch (1.9 cm) wood is usually about ⅝ inch (1.6 cm) thick. Measure with the ruler, and mark a border outside the scored outline that's the same width as the thickness of the wood. Measure and mark a third border 1 inch (2.5 cm) outside the second. Score the second and third outlines with the awl. Cut along the outer border with the shears. Mark notches as shown in figure 1, and cut them out with the shears.

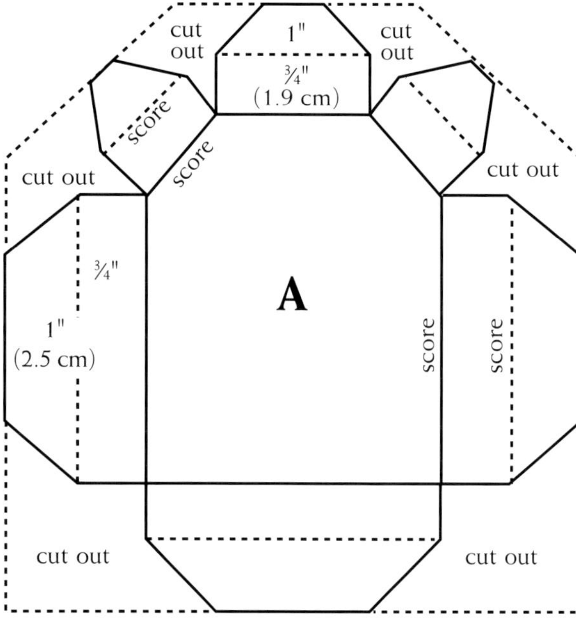

Figure 1

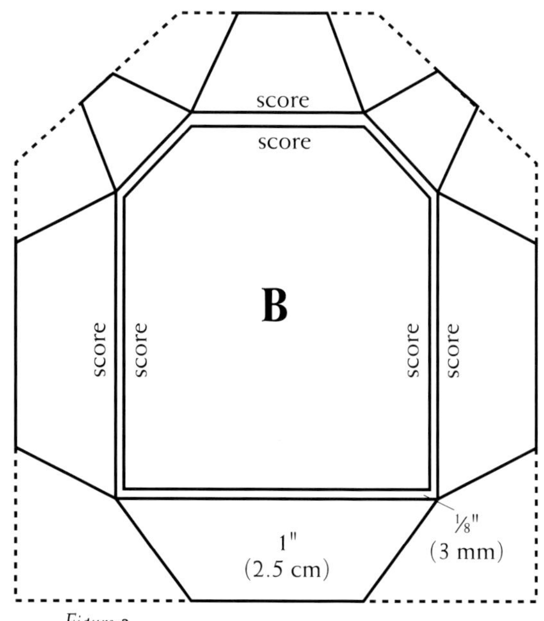

Figure 2

4. Apply the adhesive to the face and edges of a wood piece, and center it on the notched aluminum. Fold the metal over the wood along the scored lines. Apply more adhesive under the notch flaps before you fold them over the wood. Use the nails to secure the flaps in back. Weight the glued wood and allow it to cure. Repeat with the other piece. The combination of glue and nails will keep the flashing from curling when you texture it.

5. Referring to figure 2, repeat steps 3 and 4 to cover the mat board pieces, but the second outline you make should be only ⅛-inch (3 mm) in width. Don't nail the mat board.

6. When the adhesive is dry, glue together the covered wood, bookend upright, and covered mat board in a "sandwich" with the mat board positioned inside the bend of the bookend. Repeat with the second bookend. Weight them and let dry.

7. Place a bookend on a smooth, firm surface. Texture the aluminum with random strikes of the ball end of the hammer. Avoid striking the edges of the bookend, and use less force when striking the side with the covered mat board.

8. Using the cloth measuring tape, carefully measure the width and circumference of the covered bookend edge. As shown in figure 3 on page 96, mark the flashing with the marker, and use the shears to cut two lengths of flashing

(Continued on page 96)

Faux Pewter Bookends *(continued)*

equal to the width plus ½ inch (1.3 cm) and the circumference plus ½ inch (1.3 cm). These will be edging strips.

9. Lay the strips flat. On each strip, mark and score a ¼-inch (6 mm) margin on both lengthwise edges, then mark and score ½ inch (1.3 cm) inside one end. Notch the ends as shown in figure 3. Fold in the strips along the score lines, but be careful not to crease the folds or the aluminum will break.

10. About 2 inches (5 cm) in from the bottom corner of the bookend, start wrapping one of the edging strips around the bookend. Gently crease the strip at the corners with the needle-nose pliers, but be careful because it's tricky to curve the flashing. When you reach the first corner with the strip, make a pilot hole with the awl and use the hammer to tap in an upholstery tack to hold the strip until you reach the next corner. As you proceed, always put a tack in before you crease the strip for the next corner. Cover all five sides. Finish the bottom by squeezing one end of the strip with the pliers to taper it a little, then sliding it into the other end. Check that the strip is flush with the bottom edge of the bookend, and tack progressively from each end so the tacks meet in the middle of the bottom.

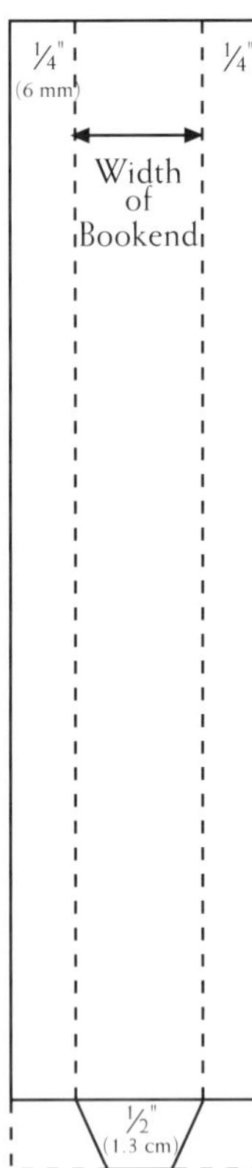

Figure 3

11. Texture the edging with gentle taps from the ball end of the hammer. Don't hammer too deeply or on the edges. Sand the edges and any small cracks.

Pop Riveted Aluminum Pin

This fun pin is a snap to make from beads and scraps of aluminum printing plate you paint yourself. It makes a great gift, too.

Designer, *Polly Harrison*

MATERIALS

- 2 scraps of aluminum printing plate, total area about 12 x 12 inches (30.5 x 30.5 cm)*
- Enamel paint including matte black, brown, and green, spray metallic paints, or specialty texture paints
- Pin back, 1½ inches (3.8 cm) long
- ⅛-inch (3 mm) pop rivets in ⅛, ¼, and ½-inch (3 mm, 6 mm, and 1.3 cm) lengths
- Roll of 24-gauge copper wire
- 4 beads

  *available from offset printing shops

TOOLS AND SUPPLIES

- Newspaper or a piece of cardboard
- Plywood work surface, 2 x 3 feet (60 x 90 cm)
- Polystyrene foam sheet, 2 x 3 feet (60 x 90 cm)
- Mineral spirits
- Paper towels
- Sharp scissors
- Paintbrush
- Scoring tool (awl, metal punch, or large nail)
- Masking tape
- Power drill with ⅛-inch (3 mm) drill bit
- Fine-tip permanent marker
- Metal ruler
- Pop-rivet gun
- Fine sandpaper
- Paintbrush
- Needle-nose pliers
- Wire cutters

INSTRUCTIONS

1. Lay the plate flat on the newspaper or piece of cardboard. Clean off residual ink or images with the mineral spirits and paper towels, and smooth rough edges using the scissor handle.

2. Paint the matte side of the aluminum pieces in contrasting colors before cutting them to size. Use colors in a similar spectrum with light and dark contrasts. For an antique look, lightly spray or spatter matte black, brown, or green paint over a wet base color. Let dry for a day.

3. Put the metal on the polystyrene foam sheet, and use the scoring tool to score the metal with a triangle 2½ inches (6.4 cm) long and 1½ inches (3.8 cm) high. Using the scissors, cut an edge ¼ inch (6 mm) from the score line, cut the corners off, and fold the edges to the back. Smooth with the scissors. Cut a smaller triangle out of the contrasting color and center it on the larger triangle. Hold it temporarily in place with the masking tape.

4. Cut a strip of painted metal 1 inch (2.5 cm) wide and 2 inches (5 cm) long. Center it on the back, and fold the other end under the pin and to the front. Trim off the edge to make a smaller triangle shape for the front.

5. Working on top of the plywood, drill through all the layers. From the front, pop rivet the metal covering to the pin back with a ⅛-inch (3 mm) pop rivet. Drill four holes in the bottom of the pin, ⅛ inch (3 mm) from the edge.

6. With the ruler and marker, outline four pieces of metal ¾-inch (1.9 cm) wide and 1¾ inches (4.4 cm) long on the other piece of metal that you painted in a contrasting color. Cut them out with the scissors.

7. Drill a hole through all four pieces ¼-inch (6 mm) from the edge. Trim the edges around the holes. These are the metal "dangles" that will hang free from the back.

8. Smooth sharp edges with the sandpaper, and touch up the paint, if necessary, using the brush.

9. Half-loop the copper wire around the needle-nose pliers and insert it in a hole in the pin back. Run the wire through several times, and trim off sharp ends with the wire cutters. String a bead on the wire. Bend up the wire with the pliers, and put on a drilled metal "dangle." Wrap the wire several times to make a loop and trim the end. Add the other three beads and metal dangles.

Woven Copper Bookmark

Copper gleams through a cascade of color in this beautiful bookmark. Even if you've never done weaving before, this project is easy to make using a simplified off-loom technique.

Designer, *Cori Saraceni*

MATERIALS

- Piece of copper sheeting, 3 x 5 inches (7.6 x 12.7 cm)
- Piece of plywood or fiberboard, 7 x 18 inches (17.8 x 45.7 cm)
- 64 thin flat-head nails
- Cotton thread in a 3/2 twist and medium heavy fiber, in brown, aqua, gray blue, forest green, maroon, and copper colors
- Cotton thread for the weft, in aqua and copper colors
- Piece of cardboard, 2 x 3 inches (5 x 7.6 cm)

TOOLS AND SUPPLIES

- Metal shears
- Ruler
- Fine sandpaper
- Hammer
- Yarn scissors
- Large comb
- Sewing needle

INSTRUCTIONS

1. Using the metal shears, cut the copper sheeting into 20 pieces, each ¼ inch (6 mm) wide. Lightly sand the edges with the sandpaper.

2. Cut 10 of the 20 pieces of copper to a length of 2⅛ inches (5.4 cm) each, and sand the ends.

3. On the plywood or fiberboard, 2 inches (5 cm) below the top edge, nail 16 nails in a straight line, spacing them ⅛ inch (3 mm) apart. Nail a second row of 16 nails ⅛ inch (3 mm) below the first row, positioning each nail immediately below the space between the two nails in the row above. The 16th nail in the second row won't have two nails above it; simply locate it on the right or left end, ⅛ inch (3 mm) from its neighbor.

4. Measure 2 inches (5 cm) up from the bottom edge of the board and create two more rows of nails the same way. Nail 16 nails ⅛ inch (3 mm) apart in the bottom row. Nail 16 more nails ⅛ inch (3 mm) above that row, alternating their position so each nail is above the space between the two nails in the row below. The 16th nail in the inner row won't have two nails below it, however, so locate it to the right or left on the same side as the "extra" nail in the row on the other end of the board. You should now have a total of 64 nails forming your "loom."

5. Refer to figure 1 to identify the rows as you work. Use the brown thread first, tying it to the top left nail in row A. Bring it down and circle it around the left nail on bottom row D. Bring it back up to the first available nail on row B and circle it around, then bring it down and circle it around the first available nail on row C, then go back up again. The thread should connect the rows of nails in this pattern: ADBC, ADBC, ADBC, and so on. Continue alternating the thread between the rows until you create a strip of brown ¼ inch (6 mm) wide. Tie off the thread to the last nail and cut it.

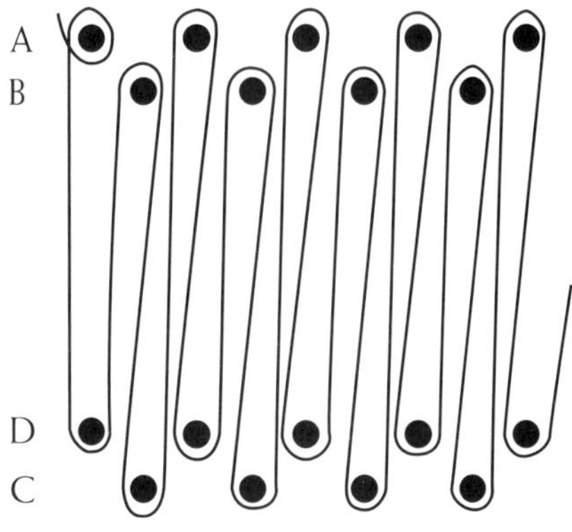

Figure 1

6. Repeat the procedure with the aqua, blue gray, forest green, and maroon threads in that order. Use the copper thread next to create a ½-inch (1.3 cm) width instead of ¼ inch (6 mm); you'll use eight of the nails on top and eight on the bottom. Use the forest green thread again to create a ¼-inch (6 mm) width. You've now made what weavers call a warp, and all the threads should be taut.

7. Use the scissors to cut the piece of cardboard into a homemade bobbin to hold thread. Shape it somewhat like an oval squeezed in the middle, measuring 1 x 3 inches (2.5 x 7.6 cm).

8. Wind the aqua and copper yarn around the bobbin until it's full.

9. Insert the ruler in the warp, passing it over one warp end, under the next, and so on. Slide the ruler up 7 or 8 inches (17.8 or 20.3 cm) away from where you'll be weaving, and turn it on its edge. You've now raised every other warp end, creating a "shed."

10. Unravel about 7 inches (17.8 cm) of weft (the yarn on the bobbin) and pass it through the open shed. Use the comb to comb the weft down to 1 inch (2.5 cm) above the bottom nail area.

11. Allow the ruler to lie flat. Bringing the weft back the other way, you must go over and under the warp without the help of the ruler, because you need to lift the opposing warp ends. Ease the bobbin through, keeping the ruler well pushed back.

12. Raise the ruler on its edge again, and put the bobbin through to go back the other way. Comb down. Repeat the process of returning the bobbin while the ruler is flat.

(continued on page 100)

Woven Copper Bookmark *(continued)*

13. Raise up the ruler and place one of the longer (3-inch [7.6 cm]) pieces of copper in the open shed. Raise up the piece of copper and pass it over the copper threads, then insert it back into the shed. With the shed still open, pass the bobbin through, too, making each edge snug.

14. Lower the ruler to a flat position, and insert a short piece of copper, coming out and over only the maroon color. Then raise the ruler and go back into the shed. Run the bobbin's weft yarn through the shed, too.

15. Continue in this vein, alternating the long and short pieces of copper, coming out of the shed at each color stripe. A diagonal will begin to reveal itself.

16. Reverse the color patterning by following the color strips the other way, going under the stripes instead of over them.

17. You'll finish the piece with three back-and-forth passes of the weft yarn on the bobbin (in other words, pass the bobbin through six times), combing down the weft between passes.

18. Use the needle and some extra thread to sew the edges next to the straight warp yarn at the top and bottom of the bookmark, hem-stitching the ends.

19. Use the scissors to carefully cut the bookmark free of the nails, and trim the fringe to the desired length on both ends.

Candy Tin Evening Purse

Saucy red tassels add to the outrageous fun of this purse. If you're lucky enough to have an old lunch box, use it for the purse body and simply attach a chain.

MATERIALS

- Hinged candy tin for purse body
- Smaller hinged tin for change purse
- Pop rivets, ⅛ or ¼ inch (3 or 6 mm)
- Piece of red tin
- 2 hex nuts
- 2 heavy wire or paper clips
- Sash chain, 48 inches (1.2 m) minimum

TOOLS AND SUPPLIES

- Tin snips
- Wire cutters
- Needle-nose pliers
- Awl or metal hole punch
- Pop-rivet gun

INSTRUCTIONS

1. First, you'll pop rivet the small tin to the large tin. Mark the position for the rivets in the small tin. At the marks, use the awl to make holes in a size that matches the rivets. Position the small tin on the large tin, and mark the position for the holes in the large tin. Make holes in the large tin with the awl, and pop rivet the two tins together.

2. Use the wire cutters to cut the chain to the desired strap length.

Designer, *Terry Taylor*

3. On the sides of the purse body, use the awl or hole punch to make a hole that fits a pop rivet. Pop rivet one end of the chain to the purse, and repeat on the other side.

4. Use the tin snips to cut two pieces of red scrap tin, 2½ x 2 inches (6.4 x 5 cm) each.

5. Use the snips to fringe the pieces of tin, stopping at a point about ⅜ inch (9.5 mm) from the top of each piece. The tin will want to curl as you do this, so use your fingers to gently press the fringe straight as you go.

6. Grasp the top of the fringed tin with needle-nose pliers, and roll the fringed tin, but not too tightly.

7. Using one of the hex nuts as a gauge, tighten the roll of fringed tin until it barely fits onto the hex nut. Grasp the rolled tin with the needle-nose pliers, and screw the hex nut onto the roll. Repeat with the other roll of fringed tin and hex nut.

8. Use the wire cutters to cut the paper clips into U-shapes about 1 inch (2.5 cm) long or longer.

9. Slide one U-shape onto one end of the chain in the desired position. Then squeeze the free ends together, and slide the tassel onto the wire. Spread back the fringe so you can reach the wire, and use the needle-nose pliers to bend the wire to a 90° angle, making an "L" where you would like the tassel to sit. Cut off any excess wire with the wire cutters. Repeat with the second U-shape and tassel at the other end of the chain.

Greeting Card Gallery

With a little imagination, you can use scraps of metal, screen, and wire, project leftovers, and even failed studio experiments to create greeting cards that are keepsake-quality treasures. Here are three cards to get you started. If you're going to mail them, use padded mailing envelopes.

Designer, *Terry Taylor*

Wire Mesh and Metal Jewel Card

MATERIALS

- Plain card
- Wire mesh
- Metal scrap
- 18-gauge or other heavy wire
- Beading wire
- Seed beads or other small beads for embellishment
- Grommets

TOOLS AND SUPPLIES

- Ruler
- Scissors
- Needle-nose pliers
- Awl
- Hard work surface
- Narrow masking tape
- Wire cutters
- Needle, for "sewing" bead wire
- Paper hole punch
- Grommet setter

INSTRUCTIONS

1. Measure the front of the card, then measure and cut a piece of wire mesh to fit, using the scissors. Set aside.

2. Create a metal collage "jewel" for your card. The card shown features a large spiral of heavy-gauge wire created with the needle-nose pliers.

3. Use a small piece of scrap metal for the background of the spiral.

4. Place the spiral on top of the rectangle. Working on a hard surface, use the awl to make small attachment holes in the rectangle.

5. Tape the spiral to the rectangle.

6. Position the "jewel" on the metal mesh. Cut a 12-inch (30.5 cm) piece of beading wire with the wire cutters, and use the needle to sew the spiral to the rectangle and through spaces in the mesh.

7. Embellish the rectangle further with the seed beads as desired. Simply use the awl to make holes in the metal and sew on beads.

8. Place the mesh on the front of the card stock. With the paper hole punch, make a hole in a corner of the mesh and card.

9. Follow the manufacturer's instructions to set the grommet with the grommet setter. Punch holes for grommets in the remaining three corners, and set the remaining grommets.

Red Curly Card

MATERIALS

- Metal scraps, including thin red metal
- Grommet
- Plain card

TOOLS AND SUPPLIES

- Tin snips
- Needle-nose pliers
- Metal hole punch or awl
- Grommet setter
- Metal or jewelry glue

INSTRUCTIONS

1. Use the tin snips to cut a small metal rectangle for the background.

2. Cut a second rectangle from the red metal. Cut fringe on both sides with the snips, and curl the fringe with the needle-nose pliers, working with a few pieces of fringe at a time.

3. Make holes in both metal pieces with the metal hole punch or awl.

4. Follow the manufacturer's instructions to set the grommet.

5. Glue the metal shape to the card stock with the metal or jewelry glue.

Rusty Curve Card

MATERIALS

- Rusted metal curve*
- Small scrap of metal for rectangular background
- Metallic thread
- Plain card

  *Available in craft stores, along with rusted squares, ovals, and other shapes

TOOLS AND SUPPLIES

- Magazine
- Awl
- Tapestry needle
- Metal or jewelry glue
- Wax paper
- Heavy books or other weights

INSTRUCTIONS

1. Lay the rusted shape on the small rectangle or square of metal.

2. Use the awl to make holes along the edges of the shape.

3. Thread the tapestry needle with a length of the metallic thread, and stitch the rusted shape to the metal.

4. Glue the metal to the card stock with the metal or jewelry glue. Cover with a small scrap of the wax paper, and press overnight with the books or weight.

Folded Copper Cuff Bracelet

Sensuous curves and minimalist hammer work are easy to achieve in this uncommonly elegant bracelet.

Designer, *Ramsey Hall*

MATERIALS

- Copper sheet, 22-gauge, 1 x 6½ inches (2.5 x 16.5 cm)

TOOLS AND SUPPLIES

- Ruler
- Fine-tip permanent marker
- Metal shears or jeweler's saw
- No. 2 cut file
- Sandpaper, 220-grade
- Claw hammer or goldsmith's hammer
- Hardwood block for work surface
- Towel
- Dowel, 7⁄16-inch or ½-inch (1 or 1.3 cm) diameter, 4 to 5 inches (10.2 to 12.7 cm) long
- Fine steel wool, 00 or 000 grade
- Jewelry polishing cloth

INSTRUCTIONS

1. Using the ruler and marker, mark a strip 1 inch (2.5 cm) wide by 6½ inches (16.5 cm) long on the copper. Cut out the strip with the metal shears or jeweler's saw.

2. Round the corners of the strip with the file, removing any sharp edges from the ends and length. Sand the edges with the sandpaper to remove file marks.

3. From one end of the strip, mark the folds with the marker. Make the first mark 1 inch (2.5 cm) from the end. Make the second mark 1½ inches (3.8 cm) from the first mark. Make the third mark 1½ inches (3.8 cm) from the second, and the fourth 1½ inches (3.8 cm) from the third. The fourth mark should be 1 inch (2.5 cm) from the end of the strip.

4. Using your hands, fold the strip along the first fold mark. Place the fold on the wood work surface and hammer it to flatten it more. Don't hammer too much or it will become too stiff or impossible to open. Hammer a few times with the flat face of the hammer, then use the claw end to make several decorative marks along the fold.

5. Open the fold by hand, and place the bracelet fold side up on the work surface. Hammer on the fold a few times to open it slightly, but don't over-flatten it. The fold should be about ¼ inch (6 mm) higher than the rest of the bracelet. Repeat with the other three folds.

6. Put the bracelet on four thicknesses of towel on top of the wood, with the outside of the folds facing down. Position the dowel between the first fold and the end of the bracelet, and hammer on the dowel to push a curve into the bracelet. As you repeat the process between the other folds, the bracelet ends will begin to curve toward each other. If necessary, curve the bracelet more by hand into an oval. Adjust it to fit your wrist, with enough space between the ends to slip it on. If the bracelet is too large, use the shears to cut metal from each end, and smooth the ends with the file and sandpaper.

7. You'll now "upset" the bracelet to strengthen it and maintain its shape. Set the bracelet on the wood block, holding it down with one hand on the lower backside. Using the flat face of the hammer, hammer lightly and repeatedly along the long edge of the bracelet to compress and thicken the edge. A very small lip should form, and the edge will brighten and become accentuated. If you see no change along the edge, you aren't hammering hard enough. Turn the bracelet over and repeat the process on the opposite edge. The bracelet should be stiffer and not quite as easy to bend.

8. Rub the sandpaper along the length of the edge to remove any sharpness.

9. Rub the outer and inner surfaces of the bracelet with the sandpaper or steel wool to give it a brushed finish. Use the jewelry polishing cloth to brighten and polish the edges and folds.

Bountiful Harvest Embossed Copper Journal

Make a lovely copper-fronted journal with very simple tools and only a few hours' work.

Materials

- Wooden journal covers
- Gel wood stain in walnut
- Ceramic acrylic paint in light ivory
- Satin finish stain sealer
- Copper tooling foil, 6 x 8 inches (15.2 x 20.3 cm)
- Border stencil with fruit image
- Liver of sulfur*
  *available at craft and metals suppliers

Tools and Supplies

- Rag
- Palette or plate
- Sea sponge
- Water
- 2 paintbrushes, ½ inch (1.3 cm) wide
- Scissors, with decorative cutting edge if desired
- Pad of newspaper, ½ inch (1.3 cm) thick
- Stylus
- Steel wool
- Tacky glue

Instructions

1. Take the journal apart, and use the rag to apply the gel stain to all of the surfaces. Wipe off the excess with the rag, and let the journal dry.

2. Put some of the ivory acrylic paint on the palette or plate. Dampen the sea sponge with water, dip it into the paint, and crush it lightly against the front and back covers of the journal to achieve a mottled, antique look. Allow it to dry, and use the paintbrush to cover the surfaces with the sealer.

3. Use the scissors to cut the copper foil to a 4 x 8-inch (10.2 x 20.3 cm) rectangle.

4. Lay the copper on the newspaper pad. Select the part of the fruit stencil design you want to transfer, and tape the stencil to the metal. Use the stylus to trace the outline of the stencil, then remove the pattern and turn the copper foil over.

5. Now you'll add more decorative embossing to the design. With the stylus, stipple dots close together on the fruits in the design, such as the grapes and plums. Then, make short, ¼-inch-long lines very close together on the other fruits.

6. When you've embossed all the fruits, turn the copper front side up. Using the paintbrush, apply the liver of sulfur according to the package directions. The copper will turn black. Let it dry.

7. Use the steel wool to buff off some of the black patina, achieving an "aged" effect.

8. Apply the tacky glue to the backside of the copper. Position the copper on the front cover of the journal, and press it smooth. Allow it to dry, and reassemble the journal.

Designer, *Delores Ruzicka*

Greeting Card Gallery II

If a little is good, more is better! Here's another trio of cards to inspire you.

Designer, *Terry Taylor*

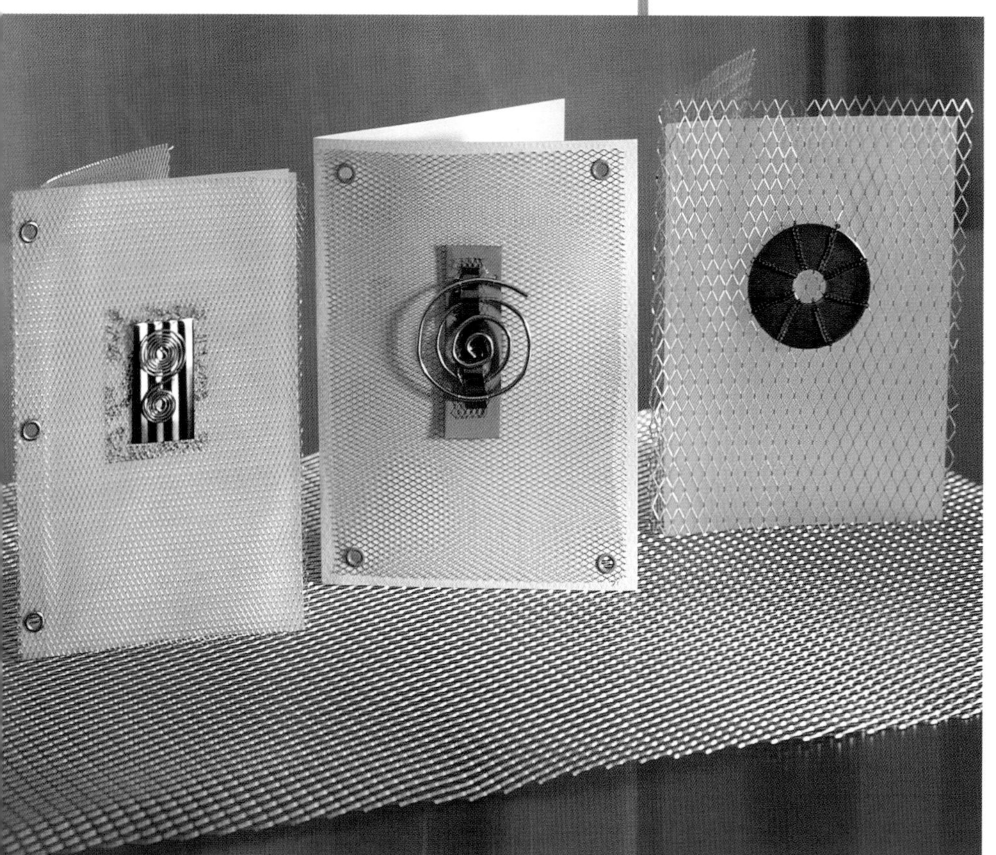

Totally Mesh Card

MATERIALS

- Vellum, 8½ x 11 inches (21.6 x 28 cm)
- Wire mesh
- Small rectangle of scrap metal
- Light-gauge brass wire
- Beading wire
- Scrap of decorative tissue paper
- Grommets

TOOLS AND SUPPLIES

- Ruler
- Pencil
- Scissors
- Tin snips
- Needle-nose pliers
- Awl
- Masking tape
- Wire cutters
- Tapestry needle
- White craft glue
- Paper hole punch
- Grommet setter

INSTRUCTIONS

1. Use the ruler and pencil to measure and mark a sheet of vellum to desired dimensions. Cut out with the scissors and set aside.

2. Measure and cut a sheet of wire mesh with the tin snips, to the same dimensions as the piece of vellum. Fold in half and set aside.

3. Measure 18 inches (45.7 cm) of brass wire and cut it with the snips or scissors. Use the needle-nose pliers to create a curlicue, curling the wire with one hand while you hold it flat with the pliers.

4. Set the curlicue on the small metal scrap. Use the awl to make small holes near the curlicue at strategic locations. You'll sew the curlicue to the metal scrap with the beading wire.

5. Position the metal scrap on the wire mesh. Set the curlicue on the metal scrap, aligned with the punched holes. Use a small strip of the masking tape to secure it to the wire mesh.

6. Cut a 12-inch (30.5 cm) length of the beading wire with the wire cutters, and use the tapestry needle to sew the curlicue, small scrap of metal, and wire mesh together. Leave a small tail of wire at the beginning, and twist the two ends together at the end point.

7. Insert the folded vellum into the wire mesh. Mark the position of the metal scrap with the pencil. Cut a small scrap of decorative tissue larger than your metal scrap. Remove the vellum, and glue the tissue scrap to the vellum.

8. Reinsert the vellum in the mesh. Use the paper hole punch to make two or more holes at the folded edge, punching through the mesh and vellum.

9. Follow the manufacturer's instructions to set the grommets in the holes.

Mesh and Jewel Card

MATERIALS

- Plain card
- Wire mesh
- Metal scrap
- 18-gauge or other heavy wire
- Beading wire
- Grommets

TOOLS AND SUPPLIES

- Ruler
- Scissors
- Needle-nose pliers
- Awl
- Hard work surface
- Narrow masking tape
- Wire cutters
- Needle, for "sewing" bead wire
- Paper hole punch
- Grommet setter

INSTRUCTIONS

1. Use the ruler to measure the front of the card, then measure and cut a piece of wire mesh to fit, using the scissors. Set aside.

2. Create a metal collage "jewel" for your card. To make the large spiral, wind heavy-gauge wire while keeping it flat inside the jaws of the needle-nose pliers. Assemble two rectangular pieces of scrap metal. One will serve as the background of the spiral, and the smaller one will be interwoven with the spiral. Use the scissors to cut a piece of mesh the same proportions as the scrap metal, but slightly smaller.

3. Put the smallest piece of scrap metal on top of the piece of mesh, and "weave" the spiral through both pieces. Place everything on top of the largest scrap rectangle. Working on a hard surface, use the awl to make small attachment holes in the rectangle.

4. Tape the spiral assembly to the rectangle. This is your "jewel." Position the "jewel" on the metal mesh. Cut a 12-inch (30.5 cm) piece of beading wire with the wire cutters, and use the needle and wire to sew the spiral to the rectangle and through spaces in the mesh.

5. Place the mesh on the front of the card stock. With the paper hole punch, make a hole in a corner of the mesh and card. Set the grommet with the grommet setter. Punch holes in the other three corners, and set the grommets.

Hardware Cloth Card

MATERIALS

- ¼-inch (6 mm) hardware cloth
- Vellum or parchment paper
- Fender washer
- Seed beads
- Beading wire, 18 inches (45.7 cm)

TOOLS AND SUPPLIES

- Ruler
- Scissors
- Pencil
- Masking tape
- Needle for "sewing" with wire
- Wire cutters
- Needle-nose pliers

INSTRUCTIONS

1. Measure a piece of the vellum or parchment to be used as an insert for the card. Cut out with the scissors and set aside.

2. Measure a length of hardware cloth that, when folded, covers the vellum.

3. Fold the hardware cloth in half to make the card. Position the fender washer on the front of the card as desired, using small strips of the masking tape to secure the washer until you've sewn a couple of rounds of beads on it.

4. Secure one end of the beading wire to the hardware cloth, close to the fender washer. Pick up the seed beads with the free end of the beading wire. Use enough beads to span the width of the washer. Count the number you use, so you can repeat in other rows.

5. Anchor the wire to the hardware cloth, bringing the wire's free end to the starting point for the next row of beads.

6. Repeat around the washer as many times as desired, then fasten the free end to the hardware cloth by wrapping it and twisting it off with the needle-nose pliers. Cut off the loose end with the wire cutters.

7. Insert the folded vellum or parchment in the card.

Earrings and Pin Set

Off-the-shelf patina solution helps transform clock gears and radiator parts into striking jewelry in this easy project. Add a few simple beads and twists of wire, and these beauties are ready to wear.

Designer, *Pat Scheible*

Materials

- Piece of copper radiator core or pleated, thin copper sheet
- Ready-made patina solutions in green, blue, and burgundy
- Short piece of Romex 12/2 electrical cable with ground wire
- Clear nail polish
- 3 brass clock gears
- 24-gauge brass wire
- Leather scrap
- Jewelry pin backing
- 14-karat gold wire*, 12 inches (30.5 cm) long
- 4 copper beads

*available from a jewelry supply company

Tools and Supplies

- Shallow ceramic dish
- Rubber gloves
- Sandpaper, 180-grade
- Wire strippers
- Wire cutters
- Needle-nose pliers
- Jewelry glue
- Scouring soap powder
- Duct tape

Instructions

1. Lay the piece of radiator core or pleated copper sheet in the ceramic dish. Wearing the rubber gloves, sprinkle it with the blue patina solution and leave it overnight.

2. Use the sandpaper to remove the patina at selected spots, highlighting them.

3. Use the wire strippers to strip the copper wire from the electrical cable. With the needle-nose pliers, bend the copper wire into a graceful shape, and seal it with the clear nail polish. Allow to dry.

4. Attach one of the clock gears to the radiator core with the brass wire. Glue the bent copper wire on top with the jewelry glue. Let it dry. Glue the piece of leather to the back, let it dry, then glue on the pin back.

5. Now you'll make the earrings. Clean the other two clock gears with the scouring powder to remove oil and provide a uniformly reactive surface.

6. Lay them in the ceramic dish, cover with a few drops of the green patina solution, and leave overnight. Repeat the process with the burgundy, then the blue, solution until you like the result.

7. Sand the gear centers down to bright metal, and seal with the nail polish.

8. With the needle-nose plier jaws wrapped in duct tape, break the gold wire into two 6-inch (15.2 cm) pieces. Thread a copper bead over a wire, add a gear, add another bead, then form a long, gentle loop with the wire. Wrap one end of the wire several times around the other, and form the longer end into a hook. Make the second earring.

Geometric Gem Pins

Sometimes less is more! Well-placed rhinestones add sparkle to metal you've "aged" yourself. This easy jewelry project takes only minimal effort for maximum impact.

Designer, *Colette Pitcher*

Materials

- Small copper and steel scraps, 20-gauge
- Jewelry pin back for each piece
- Ready-made green patina solution for copper
- Ready-made rust solution for steel
- Clear, spray-on, matte finish acrylic sealer
- Austrian crystal rhinestones

Tools and Supplies

- Tin snips
- Jewelry glue
- Small paintbrush

Instructions

1. Choosing from the metal scraps, select steel shapes large enough to serve as backgrounds for smaller, copper shapes. Shape the pieces with the tin snips, if necessary, and arrange the pieces to please your eye. Glue them in place with the jewelry glue and allow to dry.

2. Turn each piece over and glue on its pin backing.

3. Following directions on the packaging, paint the antiquing solution on the front sides of the pins. Use the green patina solution on the copper pieces and the rust patina on the steel. The "aging" process will take several days, and every result will be unique.

4. When the metals have acquired patinas you like, spray the pieces with the sealer.

5. Embellish the pins as you desire, gluing on the rhinestones and allowing them to dry.

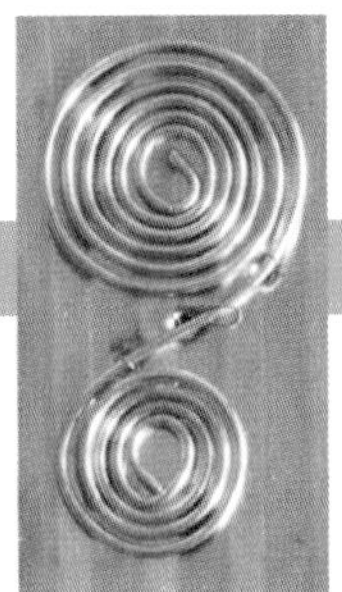

Copper and Tin Mobile

Flying tart tins and flourishes of copper wire form an easy and graceful mobile. Practice with the needle-nose pliers helps you create pleasing designs with the heavy wire stripped from electrical cable.

Materials

- 10/3 electrical cable with a ground wire, 5 feet (1.5 m) long
- 4 pairs of tartlet tins in assorted sizes, from a kitchen supply store
- 24-gauge brass wire
- Thin, strong thread

Tools and Supplies

- Wire strippers
- Wire cutters
- Needle-nose pliers
- Duct tape
- Scissors
- White craft glue

Instructions

1. Use the wire strippers to strip the copper wire from the cable insulation. Straighten the wire.

2. Using the wire cutters, cut the wire into four unequal pieces. Wrap the jaws of the needle-nose pliers with duct tape. Use your hands and the pliers to make four interesting shapes in descending sizes: large, medium, small, and smallest. Make the shapes two-dimensional so they lie flat if put on a tabletop.

3. Create "bobs" with each pair of tins by placing them face-to-face, binding them together with a couple of turns of the brass wire, and twisting the ends of the wire together into a loop for hanging.

4. Start assembling the mobile by using the string to tie the smallest copper wire shape to one end of the small shape, and the smallest bob to the other end. Tie a string at the balance point. We'll call this a weight. Put a dab of glue at each knot.

5. Tie the weight to one end of the medium shape, and tie a bob to the other end. Find the balance point as before, and add a string. Now, tie the medium weight to one end of the largest copper shape, and tie one of the larger bobs to the other end. Tie a fourth, large bob to the middle of the largest copper shape.

6. Find the balance point of the shape, tie a string to it, and glue all knots. You'll use this last string to hang the mobile, or you can continue to add more layers of larger shapes and heavier bobs.

Designer, *Pat Scheible*

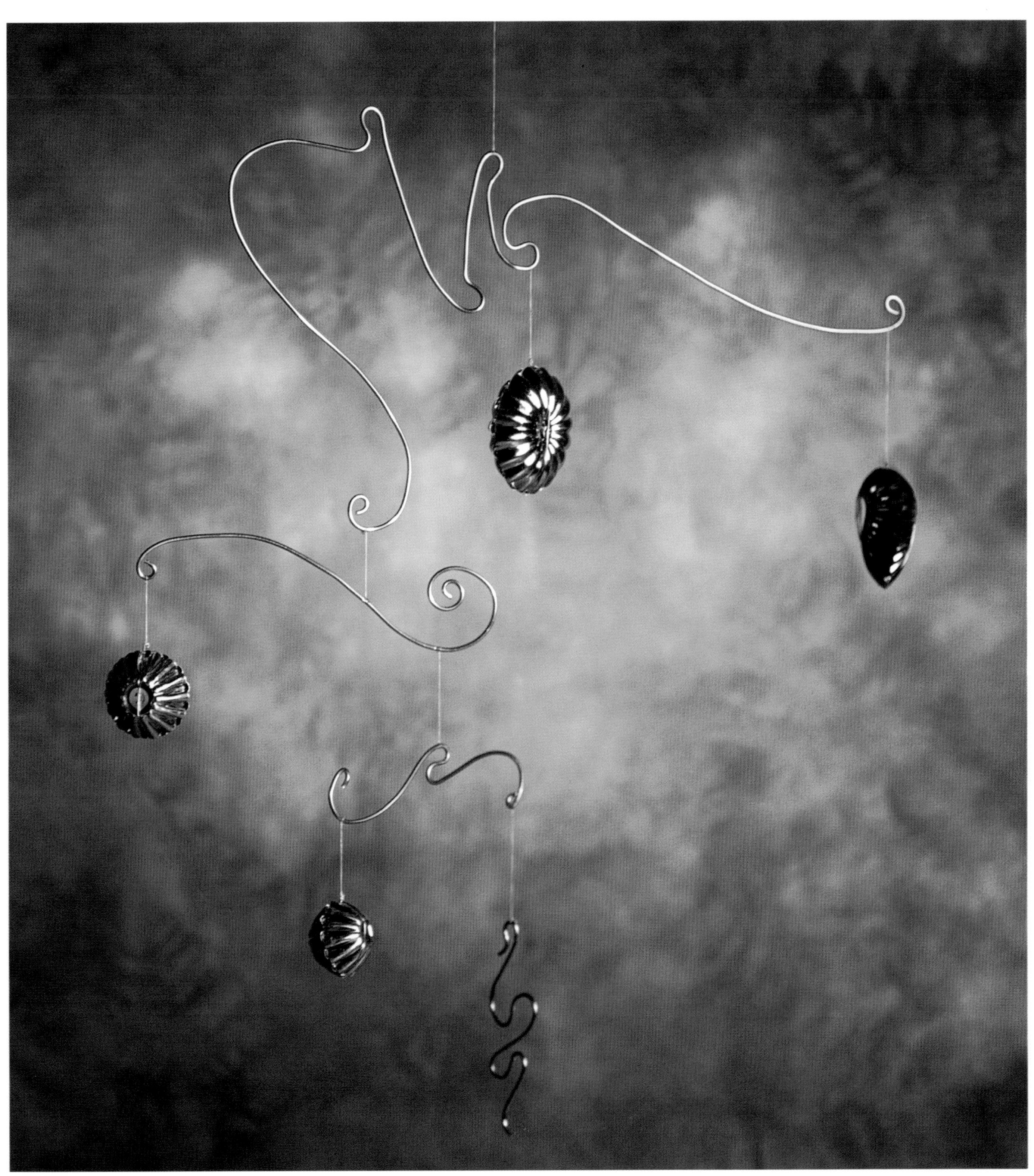

African Animal Safari

Leaping leopards! These charming embossed foil animals can lurk in indoor greenery, decorate a windowsill, or perch in solitary splendor atop a gift bag. You'll think they're grr-eat.

Materials

- Animal templates (see page 138)
- Tracing paper
- Lightweight copper sheet for the giraffe, 10 x 6 inches (25.4 x 15.2 cm)
- Lightweight copper sheet for the lion, 7 x 7 inches (17.8 x 17.8 cm)
- Lightweight brass sheet for the leopard, 5 x 8 inches (12.7 x 20.3 cm)
- 2 pieces of lightweight aluminum sheet for the zebras, 6 x 8 inches (15.2 x 20.3 cm) each
- Piece of thin polystyrene foam
- Acrylic paint in burnt sienna, black, and yellow ochre

Tools and Supplies

- Tape
- Ball-point pen
- Wooden embossing tool
- Small, sharp scissors
- Small cellulose sponge
- Sandpaper, 400-grade
- Pencil with eraser

Instructions

1. Trace each animal template onto a piece of tracing paper. Tape each tracing to its metal sheet, and place it on the piece of foam. Firmly trace the pattern onto the metal with the ball-point pen. Remove the paper pattern.

2. To enhance the lion's mane, the zebra's stripes, and the spots on the leopard and giraffe, flip the metal over and retrace around the embossed accents with the wooden embossing tool.

3. Cut the animals out of the metal with the scissors, cutting just outside the embossed lines.

4. Sponge each flat cutout with a thin coating of paint. Use the burnt sienna for the giraffe and leopard, black for the zebras, and yellow ochre for the lion. Let dry completely.

5. Sand the surface with small, firm, circular strokes. Paint will remain in the embossed areas, and the metallic high spots will show through.

6. On the unpainted side, use the pencil eraser to emboss the heads, necks, and unembossed parts of the bodies to add more depth and dimension.

7. Fold the animals in half along the embossed line. Wrap the legs of the giraffe and zebras around the pencil to make their legs stronger and more realistic. Adjust the angle of the fold so they stand up straight.

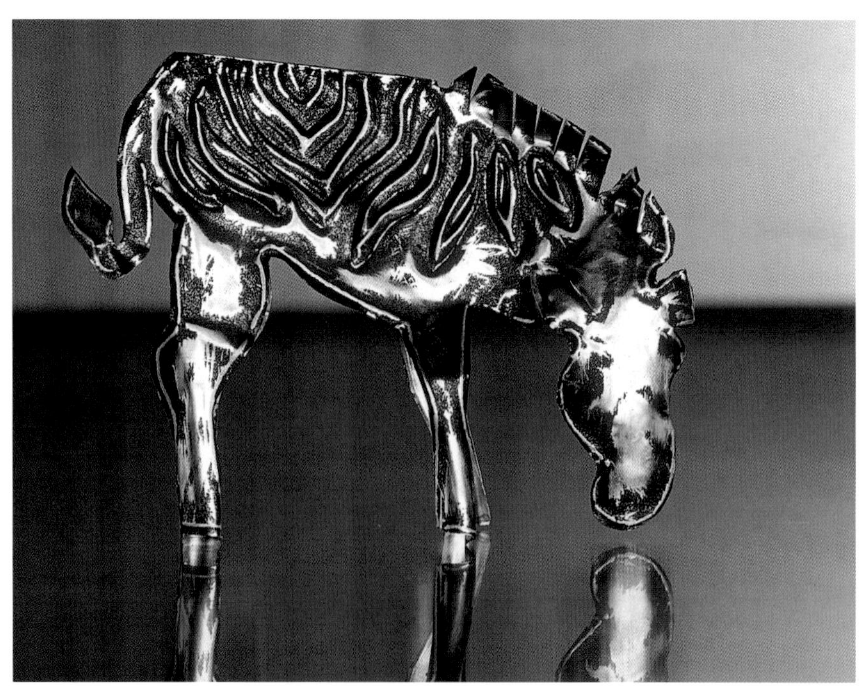

Designer, *Marie Browning*

Grown-up Play Mobile

Twists of wire, a dash of beads, and shining metal shapes created with the simplest of tools combine in this fun mobile. Play all you want while you build this project to please grown-up eyes.

MATERIALS

- 6 feet (1.8 m) of ¼-inch (6 mm) diameter copper tube
- Ceiling hook
- Roll of 20-gauge brass or gold-color wire
- 3 pieces of brass sheet, 5 x 7 inches (12.7 x 17.8 cm)
- 3 pieces of copper sheet, 5 x 7 inches (12.7 x 17.8 cm)
- Beads in assorted colors

TOOLS AND SUPPLIES

- Tube cutter
- Metal hole punch with very tapered point and narrow stem
- Drill bits in various diameters
- Wooden board
- Hammer or rubber mallet
- Rigid-sided trash can
- Wire cutters
- Small bottle cap
- Grease pencil
- Chisel or wood-cutting tool with chisel point
- Metal ruler
- Thick metal paper clip
- Round-handled wooden spoon or ½-inch (1.3 cm) wooden dowel, 6 inches (15.2 cm) long
- Soapy water and damp cloth
- Round-nose pliers
- Flat-nose pliers
- Clear acrylic spray metal sealer

INSTRUCTIONS

1. Cut two 24-inch (61 cm) lengths and two 12- to 15-inch (30.5 to 38 cm) lengths of copper tubing with the tube cutter. If the ends became compressed when cut, ream them open with the hole punch and drill bits.

2. Place the tubing on the wood and position the punch at its midpoint. Hit the punch with the hammer or mallet to pierce through to the wood, then make holes 1 inch (2.5 cm) from both ends of the tube. Repeat with all the tubes.

3. Bend the copper lengths around the trash can, putting in a slight curve.

4. Cut a 6-inch (15.2 cm) length of wire with the wire cutters and string it through the center hole of a 24-inch (61 cm) tube. Make a loop above the tube and a small loop on the bottom, cutting off excess.

5. Install the ceiling hook. Cut a piece of wire the length you want the mobile to hang, plus a few inches longer. Thread one end of the wire through the tube's top loop and twist it around itself to close. Make a loop at the other end and hang the assembly from the ceiling hook.

6. Cut more wire, and thread it through the middle of the second 24-inch (61 cm) tube. Attach the wire's free end to the bottom loop of the tube hanging from the hook. Wrap loose wire ends around the lower tube. Wire the shorter tubes to the bottom 24-inch (61 cm) tube in like fashion.

7. Decide how you want to shape and decorate each 5 x 7-inch (12.7 x 17.8 cm) metal piece. Punch in free-form holes, or holes for beads and wire, before you start forming and bending the metal. Add an extra hole for a hanger wire, too. For a half circle, trace around a small bottle cap with the pencil. For a triangular cutout, trace an outline on the metal with the pencil and ruler. To cut out the tracing, make holes around it using the punch, then hold a chisel or wood-cutting tool perpendicular to the metal and hammer, cutting through. To make a bend in a piece, use the rounded side of a thick paper clip to score a line where you want the bend. Hold the ruler along the score line, and bend the piece against the edge to the desired angle. For rounded bends, carefully bend the sheeting around the wooden spoon handle or dowel. When decorating with the beads, shape the wire before or after you string the beads, wrapping it around the round-nose pliers or punch handle to create interesting shapes.

8. Hang the ornaments as you make them, dangling the heavier ones solo and the smaller ones on the shorter copper tubes. When finished, wipe the mobile with soapy water followed by a damp cloth. Let it dry, then spray it with clear metal sealer.

Designer, *Shelley Lowell*

Miniature Armoire with Embossed Pewter Panels

This delightful doll-sized armoire is an embossing tour de force. You'll learn useful technical tricks in this project, such as when to work on a hard or soft surface and how to correct embossing problems.

Materials

- Templates (see page 139)
- Wooden doll-sized armoire, unpainted
- Finishing wax, in turquoise and black colors
- Aluminum foil
- Turpentine substitute
- 1 sheet of pewter foil, 9 x 12 inches (22.9 x 30.5 cm)
- Wax candle

Tools and Supplies

- Sandpaper
- Tack cloth
- Soft cloth
- Tracing paper
- Pencil
- Scissors
- Tape
- Double-ended metal stylus
- Pointed wooden stylus
- Piece of felt or rubber for work surface
- Pencil with eraser
- Blending stump
- Paintbrush
- Matches
- Soft cloth
- All-purpose adhesive

Instructions

1. Remove the knobs from the armoire. Sand it lightly and dust with the tack cloth.

2. Squeeze a small puddle of turquoise finishing wax on the aluminum foil. Rub a little wax over a small area of wood with the cloth. Wet the soft cloth with turpentine substitute, and rub it over the wax to stain the wood with sheer color. Stain the entire piece and knobs.

3. Trace the door panels and drawer with the tissue and pencil. Cut the pewter with the scissors to the exact size of each tracing, and mark the panel backs with the tape to help identify front and back.

4. Lay the pewter pieces reverse side up on a hard surface. Enlarge the pattern templates to fit the panels if necessary. Tape the patterns to the panels. Inscribe each pattern with the fine end of the metal stylus. Remove the pattern and turn the pewter face up. With the piece on a hard surface, retrace every line several times with the stylus' medium end.

5. Put the pewter face down on the felt or rubber, and emboss it from the backside. Always work the reverse side on a soft surface, making repeated strokes in small ½-inch (1.3 cm) square areas. Otherwise, the metal will swell and become hard to sculpt on the front. Flatten any swelling with the stump or pencil eraser. Turn the metal face up on a hard surface, and flatten, sculpt, or outline the relief area with the wooden stylus, stump, or eraser. Do all the panels.

6. Thin the black finishing wax with the turpentine substitute, and brush it on the design. Let it dry, then wipe the color from the raised areas and leave it in the recesses for an antiqued look.

7. To protect the raised areas from crushing, light the candle and fill the panels from the back with melted wax.

8. Apply the adhesive to the panel backs and press them in place. Allow to dry.

Designer, *Joan Pompa*

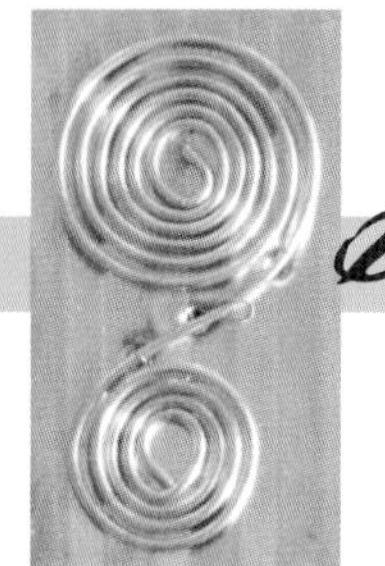

Peace and Love Angel

Simple pieces of rusted metal and wire helped create this stunning angel. You'll combine recycled materials to create your own vision of this heavenly beauty.

Designer,
Jean Tomaso Moore

MATERIALS

- Piece of rusted metal, 7 x 12 inches (17.8 x 30.5 cm)
- Small piece of lace
- Acrylic spray paint in metallic bronze or metallic copper
- Clear, spray-on, matte finish acrylic sealer
- Several pieces of found scrap metal, 3 x 18 inches (7.6 x 20.3 cm) total area
- Rusty metal wire, 12 inches (30.5 cm) long
- Triangular piece of scrap copper with 3½ inch (8.9 cm) sides
- Roll of 24-gauge copper wire
- Scrap of aluminum gutter guard, ½ x 3 inches (1.3 x 7.6 cm)
- 7 Austrian crystal or other ornamental beads
- 7 jewelry eye pins, 1¼-inch (3.2 cm) size
- Acrylic craft paint in ruby-red metallic and bronze
- Block of wood, 1½ x 3 inches (3.8 x 7.6 cm)
- Piece of aluminum flashing, 5 x 10 inches (12.7 x 25.4 cm)
- Metal "peace sign" charms
- Distressed metal heart charms
- Roll of 18-gauge copper wire

TOOLS AND SUPPLIES

- Needle-nose or bent-nose pliers
- Electric drill with assorted drill bits
- Rubber stamp with sun face or other "antique" face image
- Stamp ink
- Paper
- Paintbrush
- White craft glue
- Tin snips
- Steel wool
- Industrial-strength adhesive
- Plastic cup
- Plastic spoon

INSTRUCTIONS

1. If the 7 x 12-inch piece of rusted metal to be used for the angel's body doesn't stand up by itself, bend one end to a 90° angle to form a stand.

2. Place the piece of lace along the front bottom edge of the body, and spray through the lace with the metallic bronze or copper spray paint. The lace will act as a stencil and create a pattern. Remove the lace after 10 minutes. Let dry, and spray a thin coat of clear acrylic sealer on the body.

3. Compose the head and wing areas by piecing together the metal scraps in a pleasing combination. The wingspan should be about 3 inches (7.6 cm) wide and 18 inches (45.7 cm) across.

4. With the pliers, coil the piece of rusty wire into a circle.

5. Drill holes in the body's neck area, and attach the wire coil and face triangle with the 24-gauge copper wire.

6. Wind the strip of aluminum gutter guard into a circle. Attach it to the head area with the 24-gauge copper wire, forming the angel's halo.

7. Drill holes in the wings for the decorative beads. Thread the beads onto the jewelry eye pins, and push the pins through the drilled holes. Use the pliers to bend the ends of the eye pins to hold the beads and wing pieces in place. Attach the wings to the body by drilling holes and connecting them with beads and eye pins.

8. Ink the rubber face stamp, and stamp the image on a piece of paper. Enlarge the image on a photocopier to fit the face area of the triangular piece of copper. Use the brush to paint a thin wash of bronze acrylic paint on the paper face to "age" it. Let it dry.

9. Glue the face onto the piece of copper with the white craft glue.

10. Drill a hole through the wood block, and wedge it between the body and wings to elevate the wings. Wire the wood into place.

11. With the tin snips, cut out two hand shapes and one star from the aluminum flashing. Scuff up the aluminum with the steel wool.

12. Glue the peace sign charms to the hands' cuff area with the industrial adhesive.

13. Mix small portions of the ruby-red and bronze acrylic craft paints in the plastic cup, stirring with the spoon. Brush a layer of the paint mixture on the hands and star. Apply it sloppily for a distressed patina. Let dry.

14. Glue the hands to the body with the adhesive.

15. Drill a small hole above the heart area and wire the distressed metal heart charms through the hole. If your angel's body doesn't already have a larger opening where the charms can dangle freely, you can drill and saw an opening if the metal is thin enough.

16. Use the pliers to form the 18-gauge copper wire into spiral twists, and wrap the star with them.

17. Attach the star to the face area with the 24-gauge wire.

Embossed Mother and Child Icon

Ornate metalwork has long been a part of the history of the Christian church, but this richly-detailed frame would complement a variety of images.

Designer, *Joan Pompa*

MATERIALS

- Wooden picture frame, approximately 9 inches (22.9 cm) square
- Templates (see pages 139 and 140)
- Sheet of medium-weight pewter foil, 9½ x 12 inches (24.1 x 30.5 cm)
- Black metallic finishing wax
- Turpentine substitute
- Sheet of lightweight copper foil, 7 x 7 inches (17.8 x 17.8 cm)
- Sheet of lightweight brass foil, 3 x 3 inches (7.6 x 7.6 cm)
- 29 flat-backed, 4 mm rhinestones
- Black felt, 9 inches (22.9 cm) square, or the size of the frame
- Religious picture to fit image opening of the frame
- Picture hanger with attachment hardware

TOOLS AND SUPPLIES

- Sandpaper
- Tack cloth
- Scissors
- Brown paper bag
- Clothes iron
- Pencil with eraser
- Tape measure
- Tracing paper
- Tape
- Double-ended metal stylus
- Piece of felt or rubber for work surface
- Pointed wooden stylus
- Small piece of aluminum foil
- Paintbrush
- Soft cloth
- Wax candle
- Ruler
- Toothpick
- All-purpose glue

INSTRUCTIONS

1. Use the sandpaper to lightly sand the frame, and remove dust with the tack cloth.

2. With the scissors, cut open the paper bag and iron it flat. Lay the frame on top, and use the pencil to trace the perimeter and the inner opening. Use the measuring tape to determine the frame's thickness. Mark the extra thickness on the outline of each side of the frame and the opening. Make sure the paper pattern fits the frame, then use the scissors to cut the pewter to the same size as the pattern.

3. Use the pencil to trace the templates on the tracing paper, enlarging them first on a photocopier if desired. Tape the traced floral design onto the pewter, and inscribe the design with the pencil or stylus. Mark the reverse side with tape to identify it.

4. Lay the pewter on a hard surface, backside up. Using the fine end of the metal stylus, inscribe the pattern. Remove the pattern, and turn the pewter face up. With the medium end of the stylus, re-trace every line several times. When inscribing the pattern or working on the front of the pewter, always work on a hard surface.

5. Using the felt or rubber as your work surface, emboss the pewter on the backside. Emboss a ½-inch-square area at a time, flattening any swelling with the pencil eraser.

6. Turn the metal face up on a hard surface. Sculpt and outline the relief area with the wooden stylus or pencil eraser. Go back and forth, sculpting the front on a hard surface and embossing the backside on a soft surface. If areas need added dimension, put the piece on several folds of felt, and rub the areas with the pencil eraser.

7. Antique the pewter. Thin the black finishing wax with the turpentine substitute, mixing it on a small piece of aluminum foil. Use the paintbrush to apply it to the pewter. Let dry, then wipe the raised areas with the cloth, leaving color in the recesses.

9. Working from the back, fill in the raised areas with melted candle wax.

10. Enlarge the larger halo template if necessary and trace it on the copper. Cut it out with the scissors. Lay the cutout on felt. To make its "rays," place the ruler slightly to left of center, and use the wooden stylus to inscribe slightly angled lines in the copper. The ridged areas between the lines are the "rays." The halo shown has 29 rays. Glue the rhinestones onto the rays, applying the glue with the toothpick. Repeat the same process to create the smaller halo from the brass piece.

11. Apply the glue to the edges of the picture. Adhere it to the back of the frame, centering it in the image opening. Glue the embossed pewter on top of the frame, and let it dry. When it's dry, carefully fold down the sides, making clean edges with the ruler, and glue into place.

12. With the scissors, cut the felt to fit the frame and glue it behind the picture.

13. Glue the haloes in place. Let dry.

14. Attach the picture hanger.

Soda Can Christmas Wreath

This festive wreath uses red and green soda cans, and their silver interiors, to create remarkably lifelike poinsettias and holly leaves. They're cleverly held in place by gold "pistils" that are actually paper fasteners from an office supply store.

Materials

- 15 red soda cans, washed and dried
- 16 green soda cans, washed and dried
- Poinsettia and holly templates (see page 140)
- Thin cardboard, 12 inches (30.5 cm) square
- 60 gold paper fasteners
- Silver clothesline, 12-foot (3.6 m)

Tools and Supplies

- Sharp utility knife
- Large utility scissors or shears
- Pencil
- Metal stylus or dried up ball–point pen
- Small, sturdy scissors with pointed ends
- Dry cellulose sponge
- Awl
- Needle-nose pliers
- Wire cutters
- Regular pliers

Instructions

1. Use the utility knife to cut the tops and bottoms from the cans. Avoid jagged cuts. Cut the cylinders from top to bottom with the large scissors or shears, and flatten them.

2. Trace the templates onto the cardboard with the pencil and cut them out with the scissors.

3. Using the stylus and cardboard templates, trace 20 large and 20 small poinsettias onto the cans' silver sides. Do the same to make 16 holly leaves. Cut them out with the small scissors. You can cut four small poinsettias, two large poinsettias, or four holly leaves from one can. The poinsettias are constructed from one large and one small piece; holly leaves are single pieces.

4. Use the stylus to draw veins on the cutouts, veining four large and four small poinsettias on the red side of the metal. Vein the remaining 16 large and small poinsettias on the silver side. Vein the holly leaves on the green side. The veining will cause the cutouts to curl and become dimensional; more pressure produces more curl.

5. Place each poinsettia piece on top of the sponge and pierce a ⅛-inch (3 mm) hole in the center with the awl. Put a hole in the holly leaves the same way, ¼ inch (6 mm) from the stem end.

6. Assemble the poinsettias, one large leaf under one small leaf. Insert a gold paper fastener through both, with the fastener head on the front side. Don't open the fastener prongs yet. Repeat with the holly leaves, leaving most single but a few pairs fastened together as sprigs. Add curl with the needle-nose pliers if desired.

7. Cut an 11-foot (3.3 m) piece of the clothesline with the wire cutters and bend it in half. Twist it together with the pliers to braid it. Loop it around one time, then halfway around again, to form a circle. Secure the ends. Reinforce and space the inner part of the spiral from the outer with more clothesline wire. Add a hanging loop of line to the top of the frame. Shape as needed.

8. Attach the poinsettias to the frame by pushing the fastener prongs through the braided wire. Open and curl them securely over the back of the wire. Repeat with the holly leaves.

Designer, *Cathy Smith*

El Dia de los Muertos Skeleton Angel

This gorgeous winged skeleton pays homage to the Day of the Dead celebrated in Mexican culture. Let your imagination go wild as you create punched designs to decorate the metal.

Materials

- Template (see page 140)
- 30-gauge tin or other metal sheet, sufficient for size desired
- 10 short screws, ⅛-inch (3 mm) diameter, with matching washers and nuts

Tools and Supplies

- Pencil
- White paper
- Scissors
- Glue stick, water-soluble
- Tin snips
- Denatured alcohol
- Rag
- Small jewelry or hobby file
- Sandpaper, 0000 grade
- Steel wool
- Dressmaker's carbon paper
- Scribing tool
- Piece of plywood, 12 x 12 inches (30.5 x 30.5 cm)
- Piece of rubber, 12 x 12 inches (30.5 x 30.5 cm)
- Assortment of punches, round and chisel-tipped
- Hammer
- 2 C-clamps
- Power drill with ⅛-inch (3 mm) drill bit

Instructions

1. Working from the template, outline all the skeleton's sections onto the paper with the pencil. Use a photocopier to enlarge the parts to the size you want, keeping them in proportion (the skeleton shown here is about 3½ feet [1.1 m] long). Mark the joins where indicated.

2. Cut out the individual sections with the scissors, and glue them to the metal with the glue stick.

3. Cut the sections out with the tin snips. Remove the paper patterns and clean away any glue with the denatured alcohol and rag.

4. Remove sharpness from the cut edges with the file, and smooth the edges lightly with the sandpaper and steel wool, being careful not to scratch the surface.

5. Put the dressmaker's carbon paper on top of the metal, carbon side down. With a piece of paper on top to keep you from tearing through the carbon, use the scribing tool to transfer patterns of dots and lines to the metal. On the wings, try a pattern like veins on a leaf; use scrolls on the chest, and sunbursts on the hip area. Don't forget to give your angel its skeleton face!

5. Cover the plywood with the rubber or newspaper, and put a piece of metal on it. Position the tip of the punch where the design indicates, and gently tap it with the hammer, raising a pattern in the metal but not piercing it. Work from both sides of the metal to create a raised or embossed effect. Use punches with both round and chiselled tips.

6. Remove any remaining carbon with the rag and denatured alcohol.

7. Use the power drill to drill the attachment holes you marked on the shoulders, upper arms, elbows, wrists, upper legs, and knees. Be sure to secure the pieces to the work surface with the C-clamps before drilling.

8. Screw the jointed parts of the skeleton together, inserting the screws from the back and attaching the matching washers and nuts on the front side.

Designer, *Ellen Dooley*

Folk Art Reindeer

These embossed reindeer ornaments are perfect for prancing on your mantel or coffee table. For extra fun, their antlers spell out seasonal words.

Materials

- Reindeer template (see page 138)
- Tracing paper
- Lightweight aluminum, copper, or brass sheet, 5 x 8 inches (12.7 x 20.3 cm)
- Piece of polystyrene foam
- 14-inch (35.6 cm) piece of red 22-gauge wire

Tools and Supplies

- Tape
- Ball-point pen
- Wooden embossing tool
- Pencil with eraser
- Small, sharp scissors
- Small needle-nose pliers
- Jewelry glue

Instructions

1. Trace the reindeer template onto the tracing paper. Tape the tracing to the aluminum, and place it on the piece of foam. Firmly trace the pattern on the metal with the pen. Remove the paper pattern.

2. To enhance the scroll design on the reindeer, flip over the metal and re-trace around the scrolls with the wooden embosser. With the eraser end of the pencil, emboss the head and neck of the reindeer to give a puffy look and add depth to the ornament.

3. Cut the reindeer out of the metal with the scissors, cutting just on the outside of the embossed lines.

4. Fold the reindeer in half along the embossed line. Wrap each leg around the pencil toward the inside to make the legs stronger and more realistically shaped. Adjust the angle of the fold in the reindeer's back so it stands up straight.

5. Use the needle-nose pliers to twist the wire into words to create the antlers. Follow the examples shown ("Cheers," "Jingle," "Peace," "Magic," and "Noel") or write your own messages! Allow a little space in the antler "words" to attach them to the reindeer's head. Dab jewelry glue at the top of the head at the embossed line, and fold the metal over the antler wire to hold it in place.

Designer, *Marie Browning*

Gallery

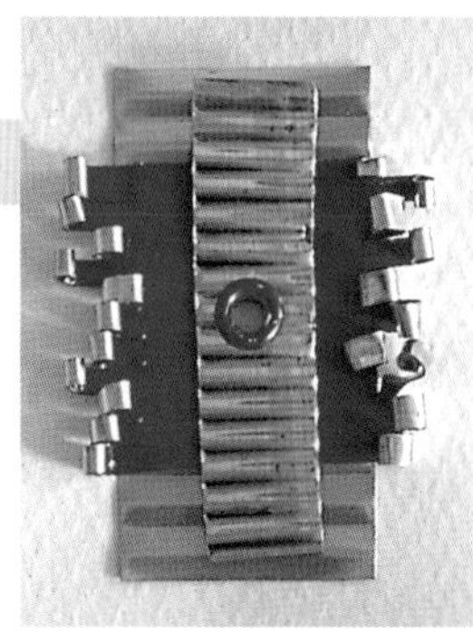

A

A Paige Davis, *Envelopes*, 1998-99, 5 x 10 in. (12.7 x 25.4 cm); stainless mesh; handcut, torched, shaped, edges tapped with mallet. Photo by Tom Mills

B Jamie Davis, *Wire Basket*, 1999, 16 x 16 x 16 in. (40.6 x 40.6 x 40.6 cm); hot-dipped galvanized wire, copper, plastic; cut, bent, heat-tempered. Photo by Tim Barnwell

C Rod McCormick, *Way* (lighted sculpture), 1998, 38 x 14 x 14 (96.5 x 35.6 x 35.6 cm); aluminum perforated sheet metal, electrical components, halogen bulb; designed with 3-D computer modeling program, welded, hammered. Photo by Rod McCormick

C

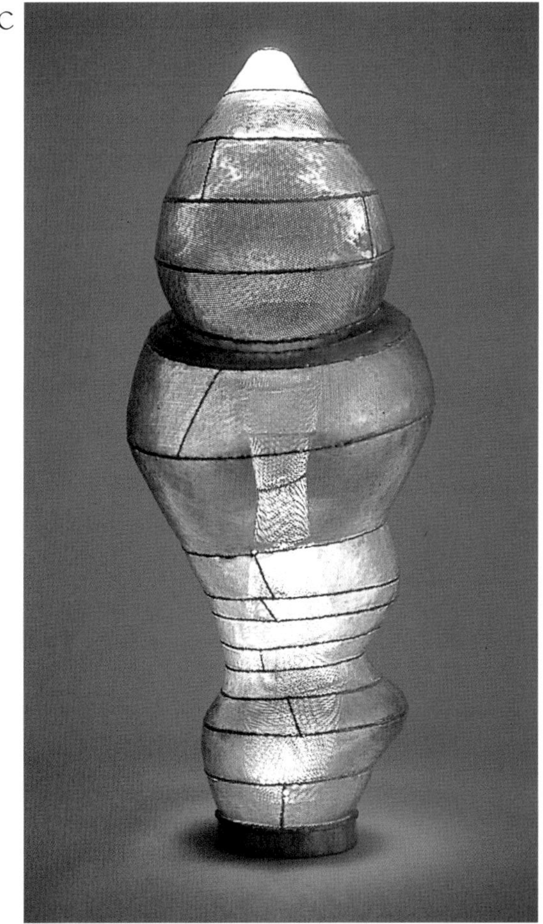

B

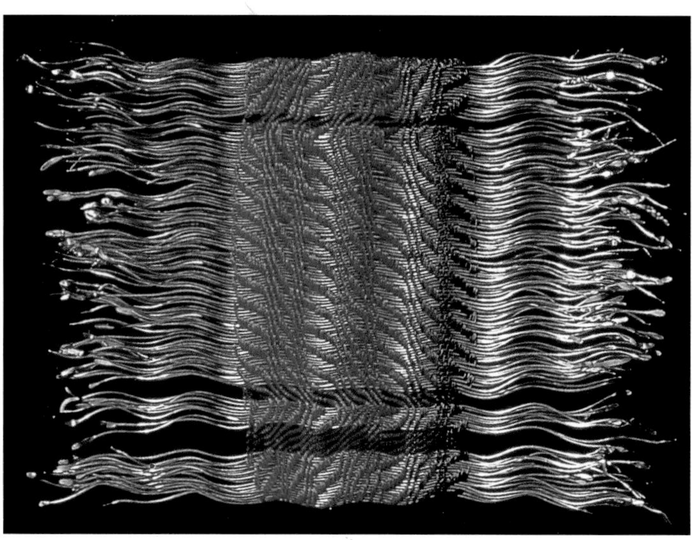

A

A Cori Saraceni, *Shogun*, 1993, 18 x 24 x 3 in. (45.7 x 61 x 7.6 cm); copper wire, colored fibers; sculpted, woven. Photo by John Warner

B Leonie Lacouette, *Mixed Metals Wallclock*, 1997, 19 x 15 x 2 in. (48.3 x 38.1 x 5.1 cm); particle board, copper, aluminum, quartz clock movement; painted, patinated, brushed, assembled. Photo by L. Lacouette

C David Jones, *Lamp Number 1*, 1999,16 x 7 x 5 in. (40.6 x 17.8 x 12.7 cm); silver, copper, bronze, gold, glass beads, antique glass; fabricated, hammered, riveted, drilled, formed, patinated. Photo by Tom Mills

B

C

D James T. Richardson, Jr., *AZ Vessel #509-L*, 1999, 12 x 17 x 10.5 in. (30.5 x 43.2 x 26.7 cm); salvaged copper, patina; coiled, soldered, patinated. Photo by Jerry Anthony

E David Paul Bacharach, *Cube Cabinet*, 1999, 16 x 16 x 24 in. (40.6 x 40.6 x 61 cm); woven copper, patinas of controlled heat and acids, open cubework of steel tubing. Photo by Joel Breger

F Thomas Mann, *Aviatrix with Techno-Bird Pins*, 1989; 19 x 32 x 6 (48.3 x 81.3 x 15.2 cm); wood, aluminum, glass; hand fabricated. Photo by Will Crocker

D

F

E

A Rick Melby, *Hanging Light*, 1996, 40 x 14 in. (111.6 x 35.6 cm); glass, glass rod, jewels, copper, copper-plated steel, brass armature, plastic tubing; drilled, copper-plated, sandblasted, soldered. Photo by Rick Melby

B Chester Old, *Knot* (bud vase), 1998, 7 x 5 x 8 in. (17.8 x 12.7 x 20.3 cm); woven metal, plastic hose, glass; assembled. Photo by Jerry Anthony

C David Paul Bacharach, *Northwest Mask Pin*, 1999, 3 x 1.5 in. (7.6 x 3.8 cm); copper, silver, gold, accents of bronze, freshwater pearls; woven, constructed, fused. Photo by Pam Marraccini

D Michael J. Saari, *Guardian Weathervane*, 1999, 3 x 6 in. (7.6 x 15.2 cm) with 4 ft x 3 in. (1.2 m x 7.6 cm) wingspan; copper; forged, machined, soft soldered. Photo by Michael J. Saari

E Scott Cawood, *Eagle Grasps Sparrow Tail*, 1998, 78 in. tall (198.1 cm); found steel; cleaned, welded, sealed. Photo by Eric Sandstrom

F Doug Hays & Penny Cash, *Gypsy Clock*, 1999, 18 x 12 x 5 in. (45.7 x 30.5 x 12.7 cm); sheet steel, cast steel, forged and dished steel, clockworks, gilding; hand-forged, hand-cut, welded and welded texture with wax, hand-gilded. Photo by Reed Photography

G Aaron Kramer, *Spheroid*, 1993, 5 in. (12.7 cm) diam.; street sweeper bristles, bed spring. Photo by Aric Attis

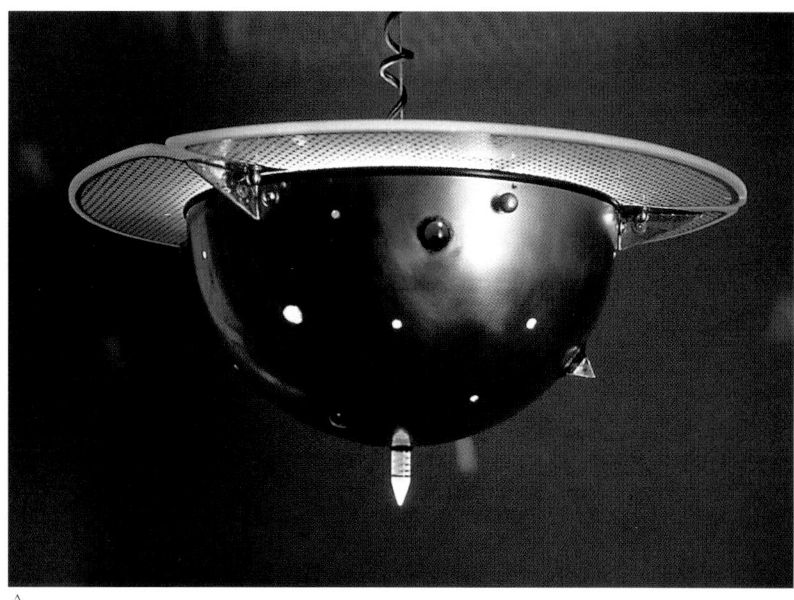
A

C

B

D

E

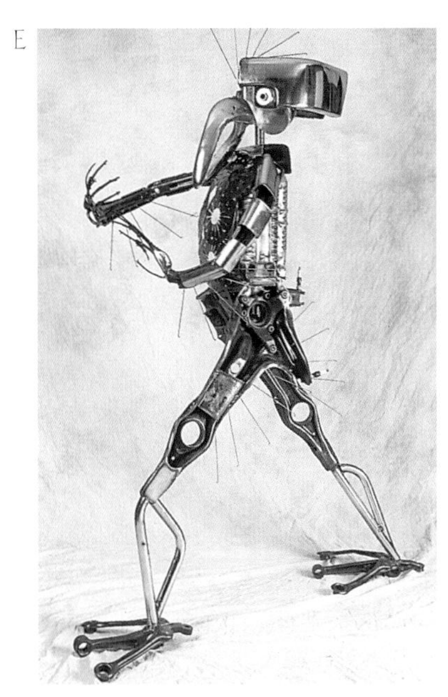

F

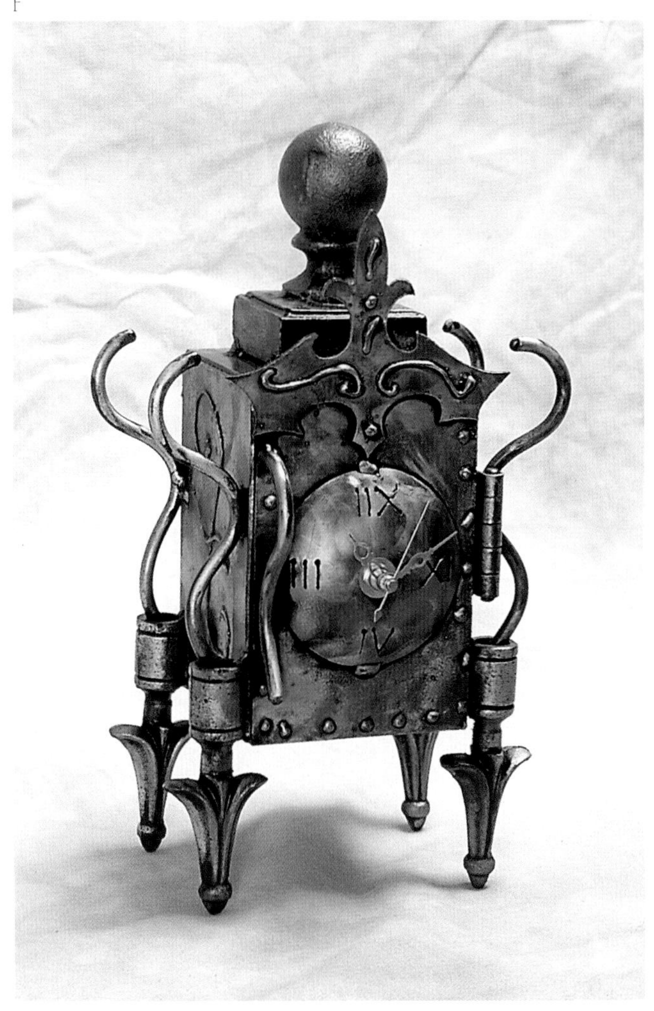

G

Templates

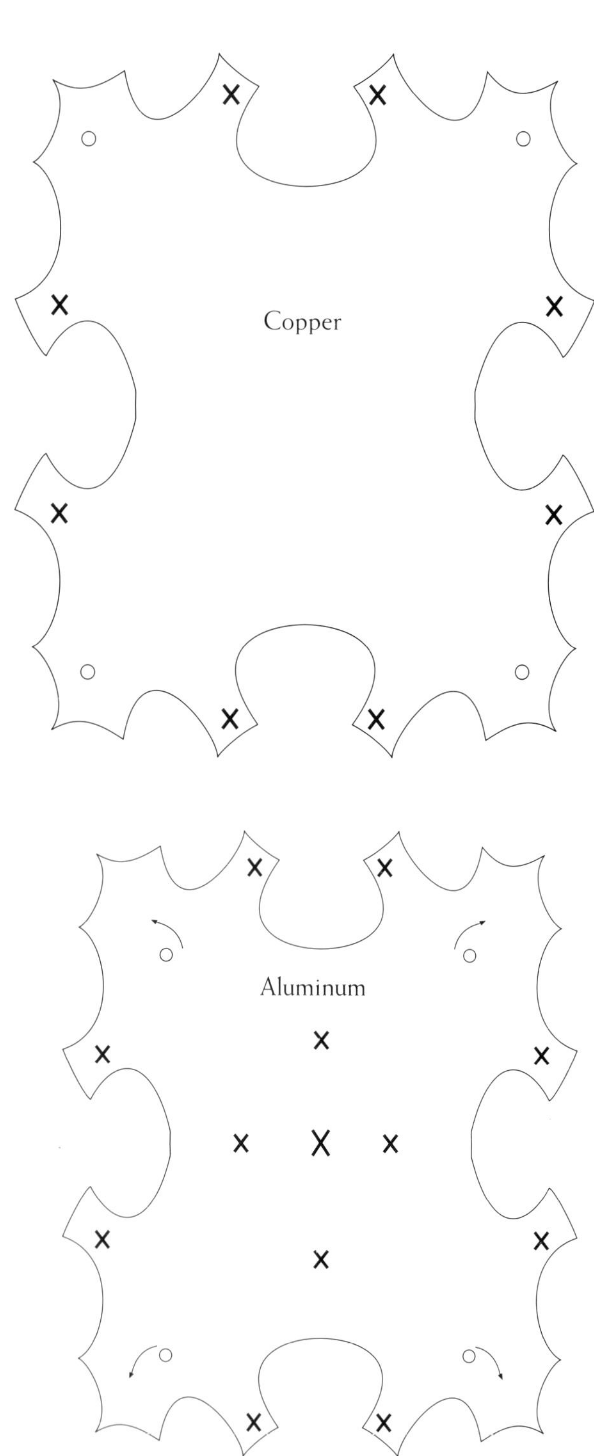

Fusion Clock, p. 36

Days-Gone-By Embossed Frame, p. 40

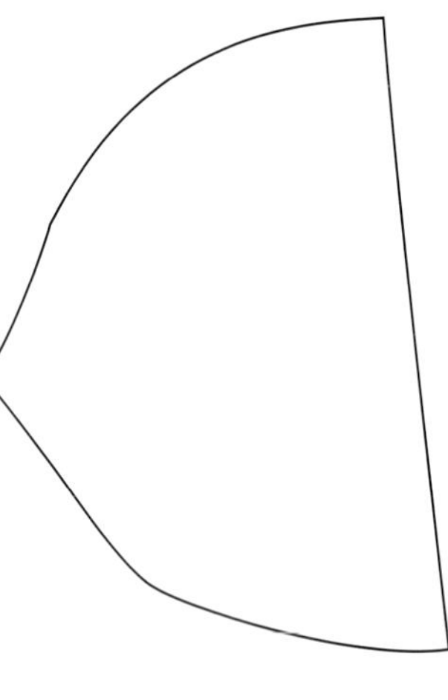

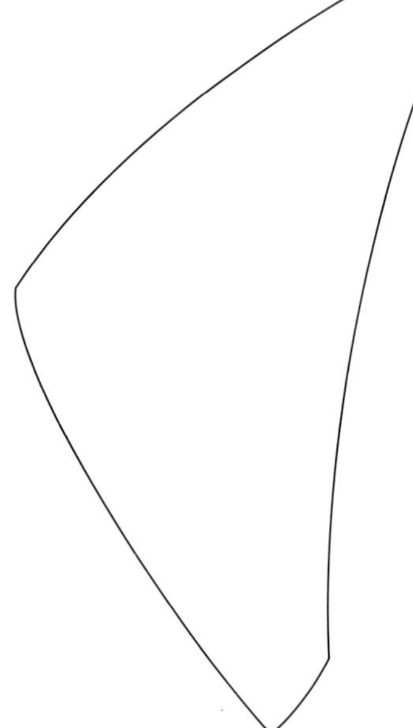

Verdigris Fish Mobile, p. 53

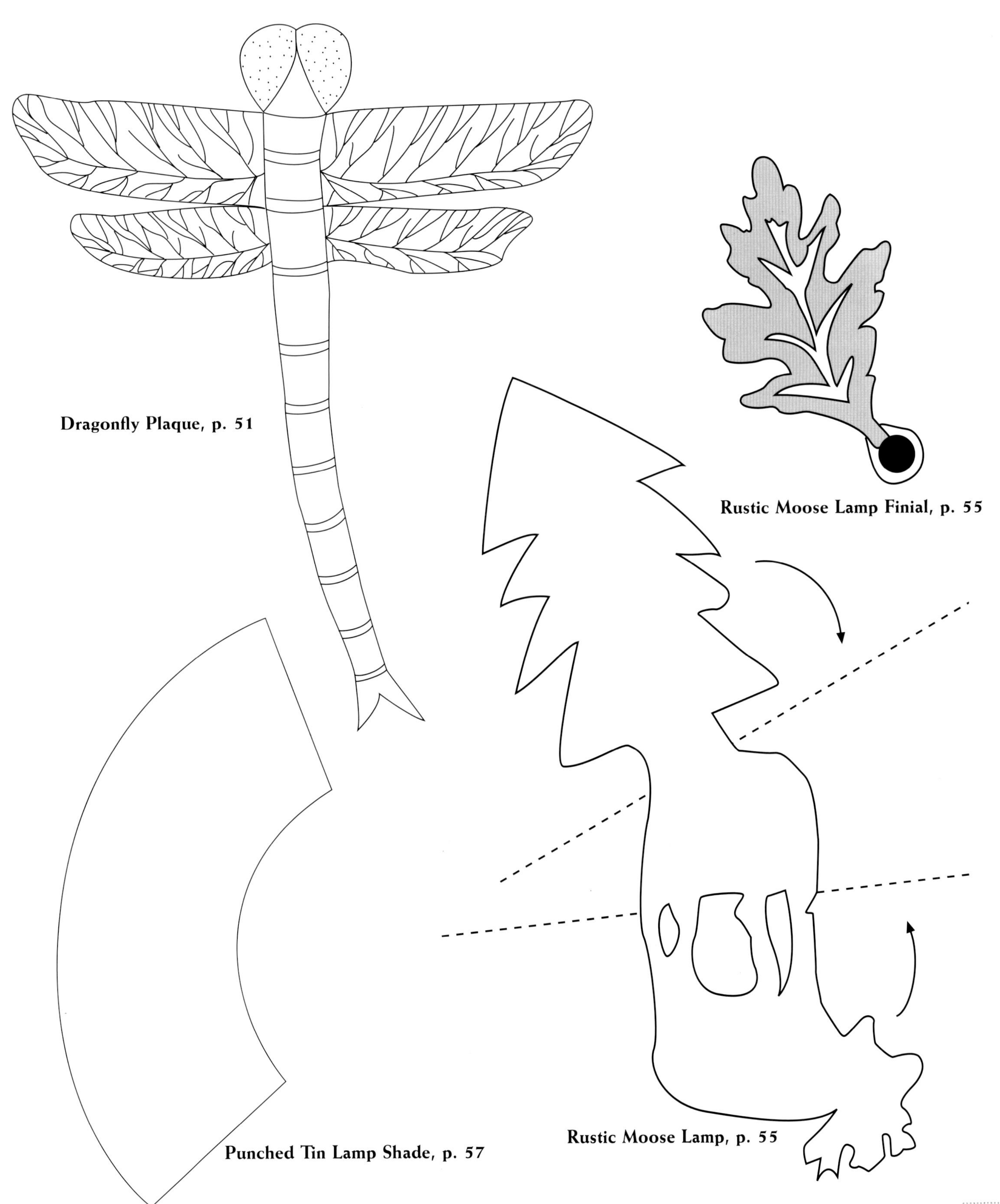
Dragonfly Plaque, p. 51
Rustic Moose Lamp Finial, p. 55
Punched Tin Lamp Shade, p. 57
Rustic Moose Lamp, p. 55

Light Switch Plate Trio, p. 58

Jester's Box Lid, p. 88

Jester's Box, p. 88

Dragon Box, p. 64

Dragon Box, p. 64

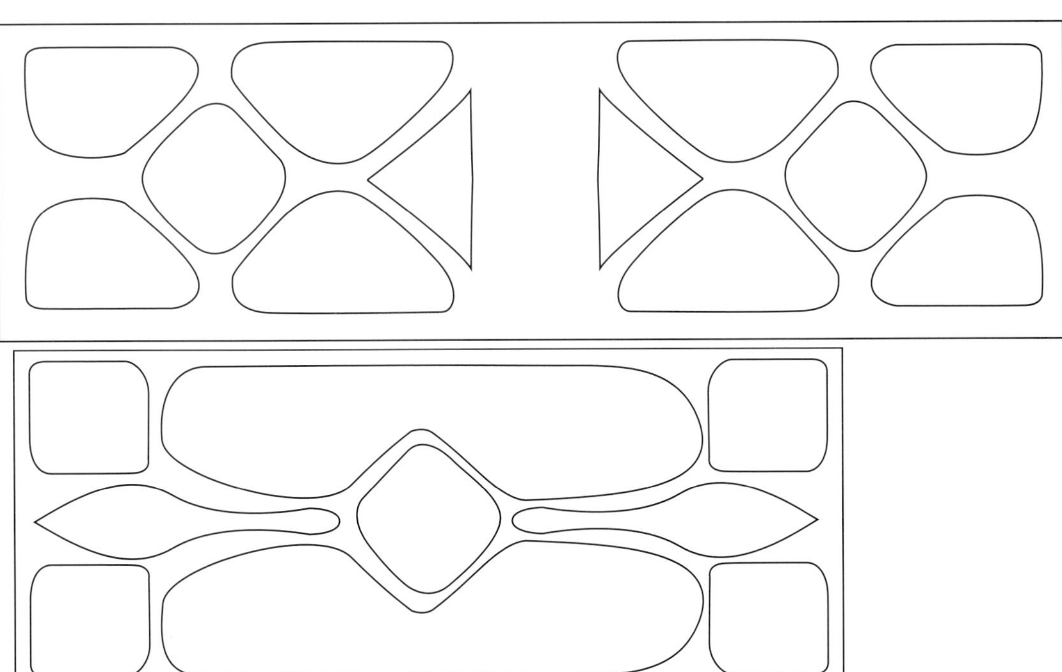

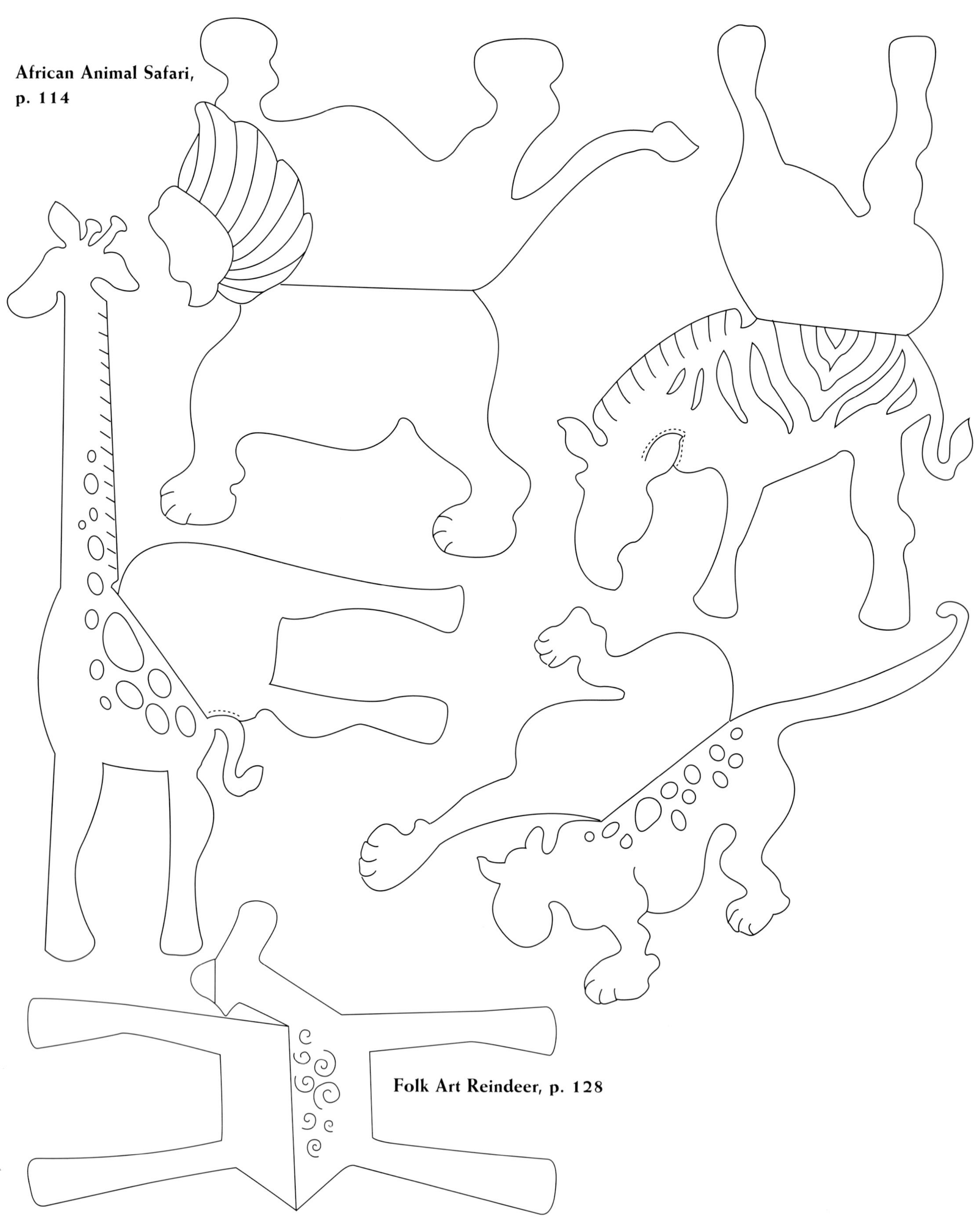
African Animal Safari, p. 114
Folk Art Reindeer, p. 128

Frame Pattern for Embossed Mother and Child Icon, p. 122

Miniature Armoire, p. 118

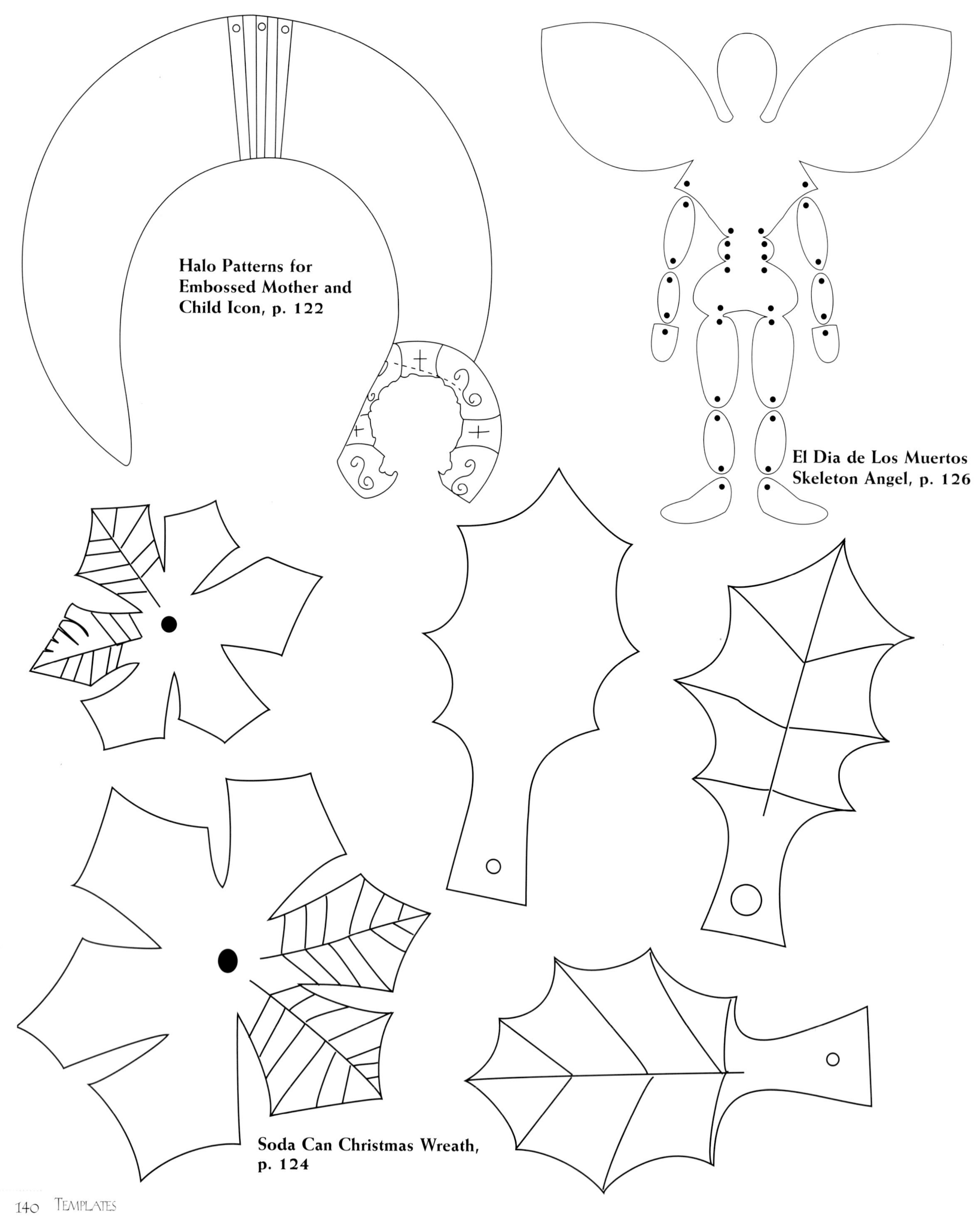
Halo Patterns for
Embossed Mother and
Child Icon, p. 122
El Dia de Los Muertos
Skeleton Angel, p. 126
Soda Can Christmas Wreath,
p. 124

Over the years, different gauge systems arbitrarily assigned gauge numbers to indicate the thickness of sheet metals and the diameter of wires. To eliminate confusion, gauge numbers are gradually being phased out in favor of using decimal fractions of an inch to measure sheet metal and wire. The Imperial system used in Canada and the U.K. is based on inch fractions and inch decimals. Use of the metric system is growing in both countries, and materials are becoming increasingly available in metric equivalents. If you'd like to know the equivalent in millimeters of any measurement shown to the right, multiply by 25.4.

Comparative Gauge Measurements

Note: All measurements are shown in decimals of an inch.

Gauge No.	American or Brown & Sharpe Wire Gauge (U.S.)[1]	Steel Wire Gauge (U.S.)	Manufacturer's Standard Gauge (steel sheet, U.S.)	British Standard Wire Gauge or Imperial Wire Gauge (U.K., Canada)[2]
0000000	....	0.4900	....	0.500
000000	0.580000	0.4615	....	0.464
00000	0.516500	0.4305	....	0.432
0000	0.460000	0.3938	....	0.400
000	0.409642	0.3625	....	0.372
00	0.364796	0.3310	....	0.348
0	0.324861	0.3065	....	0.324
1	0.289297	0.2830	....	0.300
2	0.257627	0.2625	....	0.276
3	0.229423	0.2437	0.2391	0.252
4	0.204307	0.2253	0.2242	0.232
5	0.181940	0.2070	0.2092	0.212
6	0.162023	0.1920	0.1943	0.192
7	0.144285	0.1770	0.1793	0.176
8	0.128490	0.1620	0.1644	0.160
9	0.114423	0.1483	0.1495	0.144
10	0.101897	0.1350	0.1345	0.128
11	0.090742	0.1205	0.1196	0.116
12	0.080808	0.1055	0.1046	0.104
13	0.071962	0.0915	0.0897	0.092
14	0.064084	0.0800	0.0747	0.080
15	0.057068	0.0720	.0673	0.072
16	0.050821	0.0625	0.0598	0.064
17	0.045257	0.0540	0.0538	0.056
18	0.040303	0.0475	0.0478	0.048
19	0.035890	0.0410	0.0418	0.040
20	0.031961	0.0348	0.0359	0.036
21	0.028462	0.0317	0.0329	0.032
22	0.025346	0.0286	0.0299	0.028
23	0.022572	0.0258	0.0269	0.024
24	0.020101	0.0230	0.0239	0.022
25	0.017900	0.0204	0.0209	0.020
26	0.015941	0.0181	0.0179	0.018
27	0.014195	0.0173	0.0164	0.0164
28	0.012641	0.0162	0.0149	0.0148
29	0.011257	0.0150	0.0135	0.0136
30	0.010025	0.0140	0.0120	0.0124
31	0.008928	0.0132	0.0105	0.0116
32	0.007950	0.0128	0.0097	0.0108
33	0.007080	0.0118	0.0090	0.0100
34	0.006305	0.0104	0.0082	0.0092
35	0.005615	0.0095	0.0075	0.0084
36	0.005000	0.0090	0.0067	0.0076
37	0.004453	0.0085	0.0064	0.0068
38	0.003965	0.0080	0.0060	0.0060
39	0.003531	0.0075	....	0.0052
40	0.003144	0.0070	....	0.0048

[1]Used for non-ferrous sheet and wire. Thicknesses of aluminum, copper, and copper-base alloys formerly designated by this system are now specified in decimals or fractions of an inch.

[2]Used for sheet and wire.

Contributing Designers

Kathleen M. Anderson has colored and designed since childhood, and she says she "felt like a true professional when someone actually liked my work enough to purchase it." <KMA205@aol.com>, http://www.idahoquilt.com/kdesigns.htm

Kathryn Arnett creates objects that allow her to incorporate recycled materials. "I wanted to do something that would deal with the issue of waste. I believe our planet is in desperate need of our help." Kathryn Arnett Studio, 3023 Chartres Street, New Orleans, LA 70117, (504) 945-1771. http://www.kathrynarnettstudio.com

Ivan Bailey discovered his powers of visualization while he was a novice in a Roman Catholic monastery. He left the novitiate to pursue his B.A., M.F.A. in metalsmithing, and postgraduate study in blacksmithing at the Craft School, Aachen, Germany. The majority of his work is commissioned. Ivan Bailey Metal Studio, 202 Buchanan Terrace, Decatur, GA 30030, (404) 874-7674.

Pei-Ling Becker is a mixed-media collage artist who creates new applications for traditional Asian paper crafts. She is the author of *Art of Chinese Knotting* (Li Lai Publishing Co., 1982). Celestial Crane Studio, P.O. Box 1264, Black Mountain, NC 28711, (828) 669-9573.

Neil Benson is a photojournalist and co-founder of Philadelphia's Dumpster Divers, a group of artists who use found objects in their work. Their motto is "Ejectamentum Nummi Nostrum—Your Trash is Our Cash." Neil Benson, 111 N. Mole St., Philadelphia, PA 19102, (215) 963-9850. <dumpsterdivers@juno.com>

Marie Browning, CPD, SCD, is a professional designer and author of many craft books, including several published by Sterling Publishing Company. Marie Browning Creates, P.O. Box 224, Brentwood Bay, BC, Canada V8M 1R3. <browning@ii.ca>, <http://www.mariebrowning.com>

Margaret Dahm lives in Asheville, North Carolina, where she runs a typesetting business with her husband and works as a freelance illustrator.

Ellen Dooley grew up in New Mexico and spent summers in Chihuahua, Mexico, absorbing its culture and crafts, especially metalwork. She studied fine arts, but considers herself largely self-taught. <mecdooley@earthlink.net>

Ramsey Hall has been a metalsmith for 15 years, working in a medium which satisfies both her creative and technical tendencies. She is a member of the Tennessee Association of Craft Artists and the Southern Highlands Craft Guild. <ramseyh@bellsouth.net>

Polly Harrison's artistic "Trash-formations" reflect her concern for environmental issues, and she enjoys the adventure of utilizing society's discards in her art. She likes to share her methods of creating recycled art through artist-in-residence programs. Polly Harrison, P.O. Box 642, Cedartown, GA 20125, (770)748-5556. <pollymoon@aol.com>

Doug Hays and Penny Cash design, handcraft, and market their own line of home accents. Hays Cash Design Studios, Inc., 26119 Troon Avenue, Mt. Plymouth, FL 32776, (800) 589-1922. <hayscash@hayscash.com>

Aaron Kramer considers himself a "maker of objects." Using primarily recycled building materials, he fabricates and creates a world of whimsy. Write to Urban Objects, P.O. Box 1197, Venice, CA 90294, or browse his website, <http://www.urban-objects.com>.

Shelley Lowell is an award-winning fine artist, illustrator, and graphic designer whose work has been exhibited in New York City, Atlanta, San Francisco, and Asheville, North Carolina. <shelspirit@aol.com>

Barbara Matthiessen lives in Washington State with her husband and, as she puts it, "several extremely spoiled dogs and cats." She works in several different mediums. <bmatthiess@aol.com>

Tamara Miller is a mom first and crafter second who lives in Hendersonville, North Carolina, with her husband, Jeff, and son, Beck. She enjoys projects that incorporate the interests of her family while utilizing her creativity.

Jean Tomaso Moore is a part-time, multimedia artist who has been creating art in one form or another for as long as she can remember. She lives with her humble and patient husband in the beautiful hills of Asheville, North Carolina. <LeaningTowerArt@aol.com>

Joanne Wood Peters is an experienced fiber artist whose recent work has focused on basketweaving. Her work is featured in *Making The New Baskets* (Lark Books, 2000). <jwpeters@att.net>

Colette B. Pitcher is a professional painter, holds a BA and MBA, and owns the Showcase art center, a mini-mall of cultural shops and businesses. Colette B. Pitcher, The Art Department@Showcase Art Center, 1335 Eighth Avenue, Greeley, CO 80631 (970) 356-8593. <Colette@artbycolette.com>

Joan Pompa has more than 40 years' experience as an artist, and she is the National Director of Education for American Art Clay Co., Inc. (AMACO). Two of her ornaments are in the permanent collection of the Smithsonian Institution, Washington, D.C. Joan Pompa, (800) 374-1600, extension 347. <nutcrack@bv.net>

Delores Ruzicka lives with her husband Robert in the town of Verdigre, Nebraska, population 607. She is a published craft book author, product designer, children's book illustrator, and member of the Society of Craft Designers. <bohunk@bloomnet.com>

Cori Saraceni weaves fiber and metal with the purpose of "bringing to the viewer a sense of total immersion through color, texture, movement, and contrasting use of materials." Her artwork was featured in the United States White House.

Pat Scheible does professional trompe l'oeil and faux finish work for commercial and residential clients in the southeast. Her creative and zany ideas spill over into painted furniture, birdhouses, lamps, and metalwork. She lives in Meban, North Carolina.

Cathy Smith works in a variety of media. She is currently following her destiny in western North Carolina, accompanied and encouraged in this pursuit by husband, son, and assorted feline, canine, and reptilian family members.

Terry Taylor's artistic work takes many forms, including the pique-assiette technique for making mosaics, beadwork, and one-of-a-kind cards. He lives in Asheville, North Carolina.

Travis Waldron is a semi-retired feminist psychotherapist who now runs her own fiber art and textile design studio known as Wicked by Nature©. She resides with her two dogs and visiting strays in the mountains outside Asheville, North Carolina. Travis Waldron, (828) 281-6931.

Gallery Designers

Chris Ake and partner **Rhonda Kuhlman** make up the creative team of Recycled Works. They create a line of funky and functional home accessories, jewelry, and whimsical art pieces. Recycled Works, 401 Cedar Street, San Antonio, TX 78210, (210) 222-9404. <http://www.recycledworks.com>

David Paul Bacharach is a self-taught metalsmith whose works are exhibited nationally. He is Chairman Emeritus of the American Craft Association. Bacharach Metalsmiths, 1701 Beaverbrook Lane, Cockeysville, MD 21030, (410) 252-0546.

Scott Cawood describes his work as "automotive-American" and "indigenous-industrial": "I take ordinary, everyday cast-off pieces of society and interrelate them to create a new way of looking at ourselves." Phone: (301) 432-2131. <cawood@crosslink.net>, <http://www.cawoodart.com>

Janet Cooper has crafted bottlecap jewelry and accessories for more than ten years. She now focuses on creating one-of-a-kind decorative pieces that combine clay with vintage and found objects. Janet Cooper Designs, Box 37, Rote Hill, Sheffield, MA 10257, (413) 229-8012. <tnms@aol.com>.

Jamie Davis has explored many forms and materials over the past 25 years. He now combines sculpture with function through basketmaking. Jamie Davis Sculpture, 1239 Mile Creek Road, Pickens, SC 29671.

Paige Davis specializes in fine jewelry, ornamental and sculptural iron. She teaches workshops on a variety of metal techniques and exhibits her artwork nationally. Paige Davis Metalworks, P.O. Box 56, Bakersville, NC 28705.

Jimmy Descant builds "retro-futuristic" rocketships from found objects. Constructed in a "nuts and bolts fashion," the rockets are often motorized. Deluxe Rocketships, 867 Pontalba Street, New Orleans, LA 70124, (504) 484-6958. <Soul47@aol.com>

Doug Hays and Penny Cash (see Contributing Designers)

David Jones' work combines fabricated metal with cast parts, found objects, and occasional stone to create pieces rich with texture, movement, volume, and humor. His work is exhibited nationally. David Jones, P.O. Box 1078, Saluda, NC 28773, (828) 749-1627.

Aaron Kramer (see Contributing Designers)

Leonie Lacouette's latest designs for simple, metal clocks reflect a personal shift in lifestyle: "I'm into simplifying my life. There's a part of me that wants to clean up my act, to get rid of the junk." Leonie Lacouette, 14 Lacouette Lane, Wallkill, NY 12589.

Thomas Mann is a 30-year veteran of the American Craft movement, and he exhibits his jewelry and sculpture in galleries worldwide. Thomas Mann Design, 1810 Magazine Street, New Orleans, LA 70130, (504) 581-2111.

Rod McCormick is a Professor of Jewelry & Metalsmithing at The University of the Arts in Philadelphia, and is a recipient of individual fellowship grants from the National Endowment for the Arts and the Pennsylvania Council on the Arts. P.O. Box 29578, Philadelphia, PA 19144, (215) 843-9866. <rmccormick@uarts.edu>

Rick Melby is an experienced glass artist whose creations include a variety of materials. His sculpture and lighting have been exhibited and collected internationally. Rick Melby, 37 Biltmore Avenue, Asheville, NC 28801, (828) 232-0905.

Chester Old creates lighting and home furnishings in metal and industrial materials. W. Chester Old, Inc., P.O. Box 128, Decatur, GA 30031, (404) 378-9413.

James T. Richardson, Jr., a plumber by trade and self-taught artist, takes pride in his ability to transform copper. He developed his own patina formula to enrich his work. Copper Works, P.O. Box 927, Bisbee, AZ 85603.

Rudy Rudisill makes sculptural objects primarily from fabricated metals or galvanized steel and mechanical fasteners. Rudy Rudisill, 413 West Harvie Avenue, Gastonia, NC 28052.

Michael Saari studied ornamental metalwork in Europe, and holds an M.F.A. in sculpture. A master blacksmith, he is known for his workshops and commissions in both historic and contemporary forged metal. The Michael J. Saari Workshop & Studio, 256 Childs Hill Road, Woodstock, CT 06281, (860) 928-0257.

Cori Saraceni (see Contributing Designers)

Terry Taylor (see Contributing Designers)

Acknowledgments

A number of extraordinary people helped make this book possible. We're especially grateful to our designers, the special people who shared their knowledge, creativity, and passion in the beautiful how-to projects they designed for this book. Thank you. You inspire us all.

We'd also like to thank the professionals who so generously gave of their expertise and technical advice for this book. Big thanks to Michael Saari of Michael J. Saari Metal Studio & Workshop, Woodstock, Connecticut, Ivan Bailey of Ivan Bailey Metal Studio, Atlanta, Georgia, and Larry Young of B & H Environmental & Sheet Metal Contractors, Asheville, North Carolina.

Thank you to art director Celia Naranjo for making this book a beautiful thing in itself. The keen eyes and informed comments of Lark assistant editors Heather Smith and Catherine Sutherland were also essential, as was the help of Lark production assistant Hannes Charen. For his advice, assistance, and support, above and beyond the call of duty, we thank our friend and colleague Terry Taylor.

Thank you to artist Olivier Rollin for his sensitive illustrations and his generosity, and to photographer Sandra Stambaugh, whose unflagging good cheer and skillful eye helped make the images in this book truly shine.

Index